Public Planet Books

A series edited by Dilip Gaonkar, Jane Kramer,
Benjamin Lee, and Michael Warner

Public Planet Books is a series designed by writers in and
outside the academy—writers working on what could be
called narratives of public culture—to explore questions that
urgently concern us all. It is an attempt to open the scholarly
discourse on contemporary public culture, both local and
international, and to illuminate that discourse with the kinds
of narrative that will challenge sophisticated readers, make
them think, and especially make them question. It is, most
importantly, an experiment in strategies of discourse, com-
bining reportage and critical reflection on unfolding issues
and events—one, we hope, that will provide a running narrative of our societies at this moment. Public Planet Books is
part of the Public Works publication project of the Center for
Transcultural Studies, which also includes the journal *Public
Culture* and the Public Worlds book series.

The Politics of Survival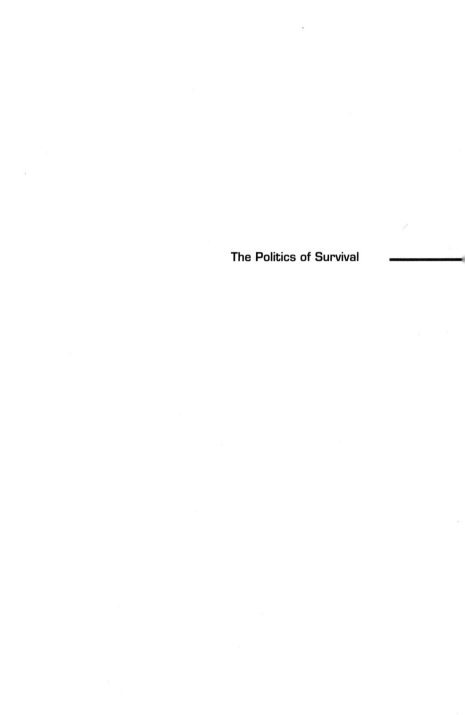

public planet books

The Politics of Survival

Marc Abélès

Translated by Julie Kleinman

DUKE UNIVERSITY PRESS *Durham and London* *2010*

Printed in the United States of America on acid-free paper ∞

Typeset in Bodoni by Tseng Information Systems, Inc.

Library of Congress Cataloging-in-Publication Data
Abélès, Marc.
[Politique de la survie. English]
The politics of survival / Marc Abélès ; translated by
Julie Kleinman.
p. cm. — (Public planet books)
Includes bibliographical references and index.
ISBN 978-0-8223-4589-3 (cloth : alk. paper) —
ISBN 978-0-8223-4607-4 (pbk. : alk. paper)
1. Politicians—France—Attitudes. 2. France—Politics and government—
1958– 3. Political psychology. 4. Public opinion—France. I. Title. II. Series:
Public planet books. JN2594.2.A3513 2010
320.01—dc22   2009041172

Politique de la survie by Marc Abélès © 2006 Éditions Flammarion, Paris.

English translation by Julie Kleinman © 2010 Duke University Press.

Contents

.

Translator's Note

The style of argumentation in this book has been a gratifying challenge to translate. To the reader, it may seem at times that the author is himself making contradictory and surprising claims as he analyzes alternative points of view. I have remained faithful to his dialectic style, which is inscribed in a French and German philosophical tradition. It aims at fully adopting the perspective of opposing arguments and following their internal logic before emerging to make an original claim.

I would like to thank the following people for their careful readings of various chapters and helpful suggestions for clarification and style: Don Brenneis, Laurie Kain Hart, Drew Konove, Sophia Beal, Claudio Sopranzetti, Hassan Al-Damluji, Tara Dankel, the three anonymous readers, and the editing staff at Duke University Press. To them and to the author, Marc Abélès, who entrusted me with his writing and clarified difficulties throughout the translation process, I am much indebted.

Julie Kleinman

Preface to the English Edition

Autumn 2000: I was completing fieldwork in Silicon Valley among those entrepreneurs who have made a lot of money developing computer technology and internet programs. I discovered a universe of networks that stretched from two Pacific coastlines, realizing concretely what globalization means today.

What were the high-techers doing with the fortunes they accumulated? Other than enriching themselves, they invested some of their money in foundations, because they believed in their philanthropic duty toward society. These gifts financed social and environmental causes as well as medical and educational research. One day I met one of the best-known philanthropists in Silicon Valley, and I asked him about his motivation for giving such important gifts. "I want to save the world," he responded. "You know that we could all disappear next week."

I must have looked incredulous. "You know about asteroids?" he continued. "Well, if the earth is hit by an asteroid, we're going to disappear. You know that in 1994 the asteroid

XL1 arrived 65,000 miles from earth. We had fourteen hours to react, which is nothing. When you think that 90 percent of asteroids that could hit the earth have not been identified, you realize the risk." A year later, it was not an asteroid that shook the planet, but two airplanes that hit the Twin Towers at full force . . .

"Save the world": the idea used to seem unreasonable or even absurd. It assumed that the survival of the planet was truly a major problem. The entrepreneur reminded me vaguely of Orson Welles's character Citizen Kane, who expressed a different kind of paranoia in a different era. Today, however, what was once part of a minority fantasy had become a massive reality. After the attacks of September 11, 2001, confronted with the increase in environmental catastrophes and climate degradation, citizens and politicians moved the question of survival to the center of their concerns.

The United States is doubly concerned by this debate. Of course, it has long thought of itself as protected by wealth and power, and the Soviet bloc's crumbling seemed to assure America an uncontested hegemonic position at the dawn of the twenty-first century. This situation now seems counterbalanced by the conflicts in which the United States is engaged.

Moreover, the fever of consumption and the industrial expansion that sustains it produce harmful effects on the environment. The United States has been called out on concrete questions such as CO_2 emissions, and on more general problems with the development model promulgated by American policy makers. The emergence of a new paradigm centered on sustainable development is transforming global geopolitics.

This paradigm puts the horizon of survival and threat at its center, orienting political action around that horizon. How should we characterize this new situation? How shall we define the politics of survival today? It seemed important to deal with these questions, as it has become urgent to redefine how we think on the global scale. Some might object that, as a European, I have a limited point of view, but this argument based on cultural and geographical relativism could disqualify any attempt to think about world changes. If this were the case, everyone would have to content themselves with the study of their own country, without taking account of what is happening on the planetary scale. But to close oneself in an almost autistic isolation is to be condemned to losing the view of the totality of interdependences and interactions that are placed under the concept of globalization.

In addition, if we highlight the differences between Europe, the United States, the emerging economies, and the developing countries, we sometimes have the tendency to underestimate the points of comparison and similarity between two societies that are geographically far from each other. For example, the application of neoliberal strategies induces transformations in governance, along with the reinforcement of transnational forms and the weakening of national sovereignty. What is precisely interesting is that we can focus on this type of change in very different contexts, just as well from a study of European institutions as from research carried out in Indian public health policy (Gupta and Sharma 2006). In both cases, the appearance of new public actors animated by logics that have nothing to do with the welfare state progressively disrupt the way that people conceive of their relationship to political power. In the villages studied by Sharma and Gupta, local leaders directing health programs were not civil servants working for the state, but rather representatives of international nongovernmental organizations (NGOs); they did not redistribute money, but were focused on achieving individual empowerment. Local residents, in becoming aware of this change in orientation, were destabilized and sometimes violently manifested their disquiet.

The changes in governance create an analogous destabilization in countries like Germany, France, and Italy where the growing absence of the state in the economy is experienced as a threat. Economic power transcending national borders and industrial delocalization testify to the impotence of national authorities. I analyze the negative reaction to the European constitution, a reaction that led to its rejection in 2005, not as a refusal of European construction, but more profoundly as the manifestation of the anxiety that globalization incites. One of the principle questions that humans are asking, from one end of the planet to the other, concerns the possibility of curbing the deterioration of ecological and societal conditions, whereas the modes of government seem to be losing control over these domains.

This is where the problem of survival takes on a focal importance. Must we assume that a truly historic pessimism has grabbed its hold of humans? In any case, it is clear that the difficulty of proposing alternatives leads to an attitude of resignation, as we see in the United States, where the engagement in Iraq incites enormous skepticism even among those who traditionally condoned power politics. As considerable as military power may be, people are aware that a whole ensemble of interactions between geopolitical forces intervenes not only in the military realm but also in the realms of communication and information. The idea of imperialism founded on the primacy of the nation-state appears less and less pertinent today: ideals of conquest and their correlate patriotism have made way for a more realist vision of world (dis)orders, dictated by a simple exigency: as much as possible, limit the damage.

It is not coincidental that almost everywhere politics has gained a bad reputation. The distrust that surrounds it relates in part to politicians' unscrupulous behavior. In addition to the well-known denunciations of corruption that sustain various forms of populism, however, we are more and more aware that political discourse inadequately represents reality. This inadequacy is often interpreted as a consequence of the displacement of power and influence from the political sphere to the economic one, characterized by the increasingly impersonal authority of financial markets. Such an interpretation suggests that political power is extremely limited. I suggest another hypothesis: political power is not being reduced; rather, it is being redirected. The interiorization of the survival problem significantly modifies the goal given to political action via the establishment of new priorities. This situation opens a totally new perspective because it disrupts the objectives and stakes that dominated partisan politics, a configuration that is losing relevance. My ambition in this book is thus to define the political space of survival and analyze the specific modes of governmentality that are invented to put these politics into practice.

Acknowledgments

The book has benefited greatly from those who have listened and commented on my papers and presentations. Various parts of the book have been presented at conferences and seminars in the United States, Canada, and Europe. I have benefited the most from discussions held at the Laboratoire d'Anthropologie des Institutions et des Organisations Sociales (LAIOS, EHESS-CNRS), Boston University, Princeton University, and the University of Montreal.

I am also grateful for stimulating discussions with Arjun Appadurai, Joâo Biehl, James Boon, John Borneman, Don Brenneis, Marcel Detienne, Carol Greenhouse, Michael Herzfeld, Henri-Pierre Jeudy, Claudio Lomnitz, George Marcus, Mariella Pandolfi, Boris Petric, Vivien Schmidt, and Sophie Wahnich. I would like to acknowledge the influence of Marie Cuillerai's thinking, especially in shaping my ideas about the economy of survival.

The project received support from the Centre National de la Recherche Scientifique and from the Institut pour la Recherche of the Caisse des Dépôts et Consignations. I am much indebted to Isabelle Laudier, the director of the Institut.

My warmest thanks go to Ken Wissoker at Duke University Press for his confidence and his support. I am grateful to the anonymous reviewers for their constructive suggestions that helped to make this a better book.

Special thanks go to my translator, Julie Kleinman, who admirably captured the style and the spirit of the book.

Introduction

This book begins with uncertainty. I was born into a world that was divided in two blocs after enormous bloodshed—a world that, despite everything, still believed in progress, where we could still suggest, without irony, the brilliance that the future would bring. And yet, this was after the death camps, after Hiroshima—a world where the balance of terror ruled.

I am part of a generation that thought it could criticize systems and institutions in order to create something different. We threw our laughter and desires against these harsh realities, and irony was never very far. Utopia was on our agendas. We were the children of those terrible wars, but we burned with the passion to live and create. Of course, great thinkers contrasted these optimistic projects with a tough reality worn by the absurd. For us, they were nothing more than the continuation of the old skeptical tradition.

Subsequently, we had to take into account a history that was not unfolding as we had expected. Worse still: the end of the cold war and the collapse of a system at the end of its rope opened the floodgates to groundswells that no one had seen coming. This tidal wave shattered the benchmarks that had once seemed unchangeable. We were introduced to the irony of history.

Today, words such as engagement, revolt, and utopia almost make us laugh. When just lighting up a cigarette has become synonymous with mortal danger, when taking public transportation causes us to wonder if we will return home in one piece, the idea of changing the world seems, at the very least, out of place. What rallies our skills and spirits most effectively is the invention and installation of more and more efficient control systems. Before everything else, our prime worry is to avoid the worst, and the means we have put in place claim to be up to the task.

Are we, thus, in an Orwellian world? Have we passed the point of no return so that from now on we have no other perspective than a deadlocked face-off between the pressure of the system and the force of terror?

This books deals with the transformations that influence the contemporary political imaginary in the context of globalization. In this introduction, I will elaborate on how my point of view differs from those generally found in the vast literature on globalization and why I privilege this new configuration of the political imaginary.

Generally, globalization is presented as a historical transformation that affects all societies on the planet. A large number of studies have been dedicated to investigating the causes of this mutation. Economists were the first to highlight its amplitude, and their contribution determined how globalization would later be explained in the social sciences. The economists' point of view emphasizes two factors: the crucial transformation of production through major technological innovation and the emergence of neoliberal politics at the global level.

According to this explanation, globalization is anchored in transformations that deal with economic production and its organization, which is linked to the computing revolution. This new technology is not limited to the dramatic improvement of communication from one end of the planet to the other. The information economy is characterized by the importance of "immaterial work" (Hardt and Negri 2001, 355): the production of services and knowledge, and the activity of communication. In the production of merchandise, the conception of a product and its communication through advertisement becomes more important than its actual fabrication. Conception and communication are the most expensive elements in a process where fabrication is often delocalized and based on inexpensive labor.

This new "network society" was conducive to a profound transformation in economic policies. The flexibility of a new productive model was translated into the will of neoliberals who, in London and Washington, began to carry out their program in the 1980s. To profit from financial capital and take full advantage of postindustrial society's innovations, it was necessary to introduce flexibility at the heart of the mechanism. The objective was to overcome the obstacles that constrained the free circulation of capital by limiting state intervention and making the market economy as fluid as possible. This is how the Washington consensus, inspiring the International Monetary Fund (IMF) and the World Bank, was adopted. This plan sought to limit anything that interfered with the enterprising initiatives of individuals, which especially involved a reduction in government spending. We witnessed a spectacular rejection of all forms of state interventionism, in order to be done with the legislative and regulatory impulse that characterized the welfare state.

While the extension of commercial relationships and the progressive internationalization of economies continued in the *longue durée*, neoliberal globalization is a relatively recent phenomenon that found its full expression in the 1990s. It results from the convergence of several different factors. Neoliberalism became the official politics of the United States under Ronald Reagan beginning in 1981. The triumph of post-Fordism and technological innovations had "shrunk" the planet. But the neoliberal turn of economic doctrine in the United States required two essential changes: the end of rival superpowers and the Third World's acceptance of neoliberalism. Until the middle of the 1980s, neither was a reality. The debt crises of the 1970s and the following decade were crucial for the incorporation of the Third World in the neoliberal system. Almost all developing countries had conserved some autonomy, attempting to protect indigenous industries against foreign competition through high tariffs or the total prohibition of certain imported merchandise. During this period, from the perspective of governance, everything was accomplished in order to promote the free transfer of capital and the reduction of tariff barriers, by modifying legislation, rules, and procedures. Flexibility was the primary goal in regard to the labor market. The master word was *deregulation*. Neoliberal theories had an even greater impact because the geopolitical environment was experiencing unprecedented disruption with the crumbling of socialist regimes.

This effort to stimulate the mobility of capital on the global scale characterized the final decades of the twentieth century. "For the first time in history," writes Manuel Castells, "capital was managed day and night through financial markets operating in real time" (2001 [1996], 122). Marx's dream (or nightmare) would have been information technology and the networks that make it possible. Day and night, money makes money. It transcends the contingencies of space and time. We must also highlight the impact of deregulation, which created an unprecedented situation at the dawn of the twenty-first century, to the point where some observed the demission of the nation state, effacing itself when confronted with the all-powerful financial markets.

Globalization is inseparable from the dynamic created and sustained by the objective of financial performance. This final exigency imposes itself in a tyrannical manner on industrial and commercial actors. Institutional investors demand their return on equity. If they are not satisfied, their disengagement exposes corporations to hostile takeovers. Financial actors live in permanent anticipation, risking mutual intoxication and mimetic behavior that provokes the formation of speculative bubbles whose explosion can cause enormous damage on the planetary scale. In the southern countries that called on their help, the IMF and the World Bank offered clauses of conditionality and stabilization plans. The politics of structural adjustment model the economies of developing countries after neoliberal criteria. Here too, we have entered the global economy, and it is this perception of imposed economic integration that produces the consciousness of belonging to the global sphere. This consciousness, more than any other criterion, is what allows for the identification of a new situation: globalization.

The economics perspective, however, does not exhaust the question of globalization. It cannot account for the social and cultural consequences of this phenomenon. Evoking globalization, one often reads about ideas of accelerated interdependence, the shrinking of the world, action at a distance, or the compression of space and time. It is a question of global integration, the recomposition of interregional power, the consciousness of the global condition, and the intensification of interconnectivity. These positions distinguish themselves from one another by the importance they give to material or economic conditions or to the modes of representation of the spatial-temporal aspects of globalization.

From an anthropological point of view, we can define globalization as the acceleration of capital, human beings, goods, images, and ideas. This intensification of interactions and interconnections produces relationships that transcend traditional geographical and political boundaries. In the same way, the "stretching process" that characterizes, according to Anthony Giddens (2000, 92), "the complex relation between local involvements and interaction across distance" leads to the opening up of the most peripheral localities. The famous image of Marshall McLuhan's "global village" must be understood in a dynamic sense. The consciousness of the global is above all the consciousness of interdependencies that structure, nolens volens, our conceptual framework.

Until now the individual lived and conceived of herself within certain limits. From a purely geopolitical standpoint, the nation-state constituted a stable referent within which the local dimension took on extraordinary importance, providing members with their privileged anchoring point. In this context, the constructions of identity were produced within a constant play between the self and the Other, between the interior and the exterior. Migrations, on the one hand, and media flows, on the other, have disturbed the order that reigned until now.

Globalization affects societies by redesigning both global economic space and power configurations; it filters into our daily life through the circulation of images and objects of consumption, a circulation that disregards distance and borders. Circulation and interconnection also result in changing what constitutes for the anthropologist—the "astronomer of human constellations" (Lévi-Strauss 1950, li)—an irreplaceable object: cultural singularities. Next to the economist's point of view of globalization, anthropology has tended to privilege the study of the particular, what distinguishes a culture because of its historical and territorial anchorage. Media and migrations profoundly affect cultural universes whose boundaries seem intangible. For if flows exist between different continents, we can still ask ourselves if they exist only from one direction to the other, from the West toward the rest, with the threat of the imposition of a dominant cultural model. McDonald's and Disney have become the symbols of the cultural imperialism whose pernicious effects are often denounced. It is no surprise that cultural flows and their local impact have provoked the curiosity of anthropologists. They are not only interested in cultural flows but also in how societies adapt or resist this situation, with reactions that range from appropriation to rejection. Opposing all forms of essentialism, anthropologists attempt to consider complex processes all too quickly categorized under multiculturalism and cultural diversity.

However, anthropologists, so attentive to the cultural consequences of globalization, have underestimated its political implications (for a notable exception, see Ong 1999). It is such questions—of politics and representation—that are at the center of this book. In this context, I address the controversy concerning the destiny of the nation-state in a world where economic processes subvert frontiers and where state action is more and more dependent on economic constraints (see Appadurai 1996, Trouillot 2003) and the rules of financial markets. We simultaneously experiment with the limits of the concept of sovereignty and the emergence of "multilayered governance" (Rosenau and Czempiel 1992) that seems more adjusted to the rise in power of the information society (Castells 2001 [1996]). Even the critical theories of contemporary capitalism have profoundly reworked their own concepts, to which the post-Marxist vision of Hardt and Negri (2001) testifies, employing the categories of flow, of deterritorializion (Deleuze and Guattari 1972), and of biopower (Foucault 1976) in order to comprehend the transformations in the mode of production that characterizes Empire. These critics substitute the antagonism between empire and multitude for the Marxist class struggle, whereas the social movements that rise against the surveillance society have neither a common enemy nor a common language.

The focus in the writings about global-era politics is polarized by the institutions that govern society. According to their orientation, authors emphasize either the emergence of new political forms or the continuity of traditional structures. But the point of view of the whole is a top-down vision, one that accents the rationality or the irrationality of power processes in the context of globalization. This vision, however, is partial in both senses of the term: it both fails to consider the immediately and directly observable aspects of current changes and tends to obscure what is thought within globalization, what people think of globalization, and the manner in which the collective imaginary redefines the political question in contemporary societies. Here, there is a specific field site for the anthropologist, and this is why I have concentrated on these questions.

To be clear: I am not constructing a grand narrative that would offer the key to understanding globalization. I am trying to show how our representations of politics have been transformed and how they now sketch what we can call, in Koselleck's terms (2004 [1979]), a new horizon of expectation, or, in reference to Foucault's concept (1984), how they problematize the contemporary political field. In order to achieve this goal, I consider a set of particularly significant phenomena, giving special importance to the precautionary principle and the rise in power of nongovernmental organizations (NGOs). Social insecurity and environmental risk are two distinct and objective consequences of the functioning of the economy in contemporary capitalism. Both have given rise to important sociological work (e.g., Beck 1992, Castel 2003). Taking into account these analyses of precariousness and risk, this book focuses on the anxieties and fears that the consequences of globalization provoke. These consequences lead populations of very different origins to react to what they see as an attack on their future. When I highlight the prominent place that insecurity and risk have recently taken, I situate myself in the perspective of representations and imaginaries. It is clear from the work done on environmental risk, on the one hand, and urban insecurity, on the other, that we cannot conflate these two phenomena. But I am interested in the way in which these questions are associated in the collective imaginary and how this association ends up constructing a representation of politics oriented toward the question of survival.

In order to comprehend this epistemic shift that transforms the political imaginary, I introduce the conceptual dichotomy between convivance (harmoniously living together) and survival. I found the neological construction of these two concepts indispensable in my quest to cast light on the transformation we are experiencing. Since the seventeenth century and the generalization of ideas about the social contract and civil status, an interrogation about "living together" (*l'être ensemble*) has been at the center of political philosophy, as a focal reflection on the conditions of being together, on the means to put into place to assure a harmonious society, and on the definition of this society. It is the same exigency that oriented until recently most political platforms. I wanted to find a term that would illustrate the coherence of this representation of politics, articulated around several ideas: the idea that humans attempt to "make society" by moving beyond individual interests, the idea that they strive to construct a coherent whole of this society, and the idea that it is possible to continually better the conditions of being together.   11

The term *convivance* seemed the most adequate for this task. Convivance comes from the Latin, *cum vivere*, literally "living together"; convivance implies the possibility of realizing harmony between beings within society.[1] It is distinguished from the idea of *convivialité* (a term borrowed from English and introduced in French in the nineteenth century) which has a festive tone, whereas convivance relates to the more mundane experience of community life. The term was more recently picked up by Paul Gilroy (2004, xi), who uses it to designate a peaceful and dynamic multicultural society. Conviviality is a normative concept whereas convivance is an analytic concept designating the regime of values that had durably oriented political thought and action of the Moderns.

1. Let me add some precision: this definition of convivance differs also from the Spanish term *convivencia*, used to describe the situation of nostalgic conviviality of pre-Reconquista Spain, when Jews, Muslims, and Catholics lived in relative peace.

Entering the era of neoliberal globalization, a profound change occurred. We often envisage neoliberalism as the product of a set of economic measures destined to encourage free exchange and competition through deregulation, tariff elimination, and various measures meant to favor large businesses, accentuating the gap between rich and poor countries. We often neglect the central aspect of these empirical changes: the political rationale that structures these measures and submits the state to the exigencies of the market, which corresponds to the crumbling of the welfare state and a profound transformation in what Foucault refers to as "governmentality." He insists on the modern focus on power over life and examines both the techniques through which biopower is solidified as well as the modes of subjectivation that are constructed in the relation between the governing and the governed. The question of life becomes the central issue in this context. The most important contribution in Foucault's analysis from his Collège de France lectures of 1978 and 1979 is to show that neoliberalism is not only a new age of the economy characterized by the triumph of financial capital and free-market values, but moreover a reconfiguration of governmentality, now focused on the *bios*. This dimension was illustrated by Giorgio Agamben (1998), whose arguments aim to articulate the notions of biopower and sovereignty. But there is a difference in size between these two concepts of biopower. For Foucault, the emergence of biopolitics is the product of a history marked by the decline of juridical mechanisms that characterize sovereignty and the rise of mechanisms of power oriented toward the living individual.

Agamben, however, cannot dismiss the concept of sovereignty, which for Foucault is nothing more than a historical accident. The articulation between life and sovereignty is the very condition of politics. Agamben, by privileging the figure of *homo sacer*, dehistoricizes biopower; as he indicates, "The inclusion of bare life in the political realm constitutes the original—if concealed—nucleus of power" (Agamben 1998, 6). The constitution of bare life is at the foundation of the political sphere. This state of exception today becomes the rule, and this is what Agamben explores.

We can criticize Agamben's theoretical apparatus, insofar as it posits sovereignty as an essential issue, whereas Foucault struggled to show the limits of this concept, criticizing the legalism that, according to him, constitutes a major epistemological obstacle in understanding governmentality. Furthermore, Agamben's philosophy tends to offer a metaphysical thrust to the dialectic between bare life and sovereignty, which runs counter to Foucault's efforts to understand the epistemic ruptures that characterize human history.

For my own sake, I am somewhat skeptical about the Agambenian fetishization of sovereignty. By contrast, I agree with the Foucaldian critique of this concept and with his genealogical approach to the issue of power. It is in the continuation of the Foucaldian perspective that this book is situated. I introduce the concept of survival to understand the effects of the interiorization of the neoliberal moment in the contemporary political imaginary. As we shall see, survival is primarily part of a representation; it does not have the same ontological status as bare life. This book consists of tracking this representation and its impact on the political process.

Much has been written about governmentality, new control mechanisms, the margins of the state, and the generalization of the state of exception. The literature examining politics focuses most often on the state and the exercise of governmentality. At first glance, the frameworks of political action have not evolved: governments, parties, national frames of reference—everything seems quite stable. And yet there is a proliferation of organisms and organizations that belong to a deterritorialized horizon, illustrated by the emergence of new sites where we treat and debate world affairs: conferences and forums where the main characters are no longer restricted to accredited state representatives, but where the nongovernmental element shows itself in the full light of day.

From there we see civil society's affirmation when confronted with the elite's political stronghold; there was only a small step that some happily took, only to be quickly arraigned with enthusiasm by the advocates of a more classical vision of international relations, conceived as state affairs. Without going into the debate that has persisted for the last few years between those for whom globalization marks the end of the nation-state and their adversaries, it seems to me that the analysis in terms of institutions and actors can only imperfectly account for what has profoundly changed over the last fifteen years.

In this situation we have progressively witnessed the emergence of a new regime of governmentality that, without substituting for the traditional forms of the state, has taken charge of the preoccupations that concern the question of survival. Globalization has a political dimension whose institutional concretization—the rise in power of transnational organizations—is both the most visible and the most superficial aspect.

The hypothesis that I propose in this book is that the emergence of a new transnational scene is above all the effect—and not the cause—of an unprecedented transformation in our relationship to the political realm. This relationship is now played out around a representation that puts the preoccupation with living and surviving—what I refer to as survival—at the heart of political action. Moving backward from a tradition that places harmoniously living together (convivance) as the highest aim of social beings, the political field finds itself overrun by a gnawing interrogation concerning the uncertainty and threats that the future possesses.

This uncertainty awakens an anxiety over the durability of a humanity perceived as precarious because of its self-produced dangers, as much for nature as for culture. Symptomatic of this current state of affairs is the consensus regarding the precautionary principle, as well as the fact that what once was part of societal debate has now become central in political controversy. It is now the idea of survival that orients our concerns and choices through the reshaping of the public sphere. Like the English word *survival*, the French *survie* designates a present and retrospective state (being alive, as on the battlefield, when everyone around you has died), while I use survival to emphasize the prospective aim that polarizes the political imaginary around the future conditions of pre-serving life.

There are no longer single protective powers, long em-bodied by the monarch or more recently by the welfare state, that make life safe. The question of survival, which as we shall see has been central in states distant from our own, only made sense at the individual level. But survival has returned to the forefront, carried by the uncertainty of time, and has called into question the logics of convivance. Survival is in-separable from the neoliberal structure of governmentality; in the contemporary political imaginary, survival expresses its biopolitical dimension. The intense ambivalence of ex-tremes, between opulence and abject poverty, between the order reserved for the wealthy and the storm of violence everywhere else, added to the raw illumination of a world without promise. In addition, the depletion of natural re-sources, global warming, and other disastrous consequences of the commoditization, waste, and excess of neoliberalism are reflected in the political imaginary. The rise of ecological issues and the sharpness of environmental conflicts show to what extent the problem of survival is on the agenda. In her work on the environmental conflict in India, Vandana Shiva illustrates these preoccupations by lauding a "politics of sur-vival" that prioritizes ecological emergency (Shiva 1991).

It is no coincidence that interest in humanitarian ques-tions has become increasingly shrill in recent times. The ghost of radical evil—long kept on the margins in the unsaid of the postwar when the word of the hour was *reconstruction*—has made a harsh comeback. This spurred the resurgence of

Holocaust remembrance, as well as an ethic of solicitude as a substitute for the rhetoric of social change and the ideal of a better world. It is in this context that NGOs took a central role, displaying their nonaffiliation as a necessary attribute in order to take on the role of human rights guarantor.

The NGOs' rise in power and the appearance of new transnational political places only makes sense when connected to the problematic of survival. The ideas of justice and rights that prevail in this universe only find their rest in the perspectives of risk and precaution. It is not a coincidence that the theme of sustainability has come to shape development discourse, becoming completely intertwined with the claims of inequality and the relationship between power and society. The NGO phenomenon had such an impact because these organizations promoted not only a policy but also an *economy* of survival, the principles of which cannot be reduced to those that govern the politics of convivance.

Global-politics thus invented itself in the transnational dimension. By "global-politics," I am not referring to a supra-state form that superimposes itself on already existent powers, but rather to the conjugation of modes of action which, functioning at the global level, throw us into a regime of anticipation. Global-politics must not be thought of in terms of power relations, as we would only confuse it with the traditional space of international relations which, as we can imagine, did not suddenly transform itself by the miracle of some magic wand. State diplomacy remains aware of its prerogatives. What progressively intrudes next to state mechanisms has strictly nothing to do with an overarching power.

We can even show to what point global-politics is dependent on nation-state strategies. As the impact of initiatives related to the economy of survival show, however, global-politics imposes its own regime and places under pressure the powers that control it only imperfectly.

Uncertainty has become our fate. It may seem strange that this worldly state spurs innovation and the creation of other possibilities, or that it exudes unseen powers. The change of scale provokes other ways of coming together, and the anthropologist greedily observes such grand rituals that generate

collective anxiety. In a world that we thought was completely subjected to the tyranny of the market, the strong comeback of charitable giving is inseparable from the economy of survival's own dynamics.[2] Practices that mix the most advanced technology with the beliefs of another era aim to exorcise the specter of great catastrophes. Drawing the figure of global-politics and emphasizing the polarity between survival and convivance, I suggest that we have entered a new era where the politics of survival has become the regime under which we experience both our relation to the collectivity and our insertion in nature.

In such a context, is there still a possibility for optimistic ideas about the future, which Ernest Bloch (1986) called the Hope Principle, placing himself in a utopian vision, as the generator of a better world? One of his main critics, Hans

2. The rise of a philanthropist movement among the nouveaux riches in the Silicon Valley (Abélès 2002) illustrates the close link between new caritative enterprises and venture capitalism.

Jonas (1990 [1979]), opposed this conception of the world with the Responsibility Principle, by highlighting the extent to which utopian visions could have destructive effects, in particular regarding the ecological realm, a realm mistreated by governments claiming a Marxist orientation.

The fact that this language of utopia, centered on progress, no longer finds a direct echo in the political imaginary does not imply that we must give up and lock ourselves into a fatalist vision of history, but rather that we must take into account the weight of this political imaginary in order to engage in a critique of neoliberal power. In addition, this prospective outlook that privileges the question of survival is far from being incompatible with a utopian vision. Walter Benjamin, one of the principle thinkers of utopian thought, was a great fighter against the idea of progress. In 1940, during the torment of World War II and a short time before taking his own life, Benjamin wrote a text that highlights to what extent progress can lead to disaster. In the Benjaminian vocabulary, words such as *disaster*, *catastrophe*, *destruction*, and *deluge* all designate the steamroller of fascism that results precisely in the all-powerfulness of the techniques and ideology of progress (Benjamin 2002 [1940]). The allegory of the impotent angel of history when confronted with the storm runs against the conception of a liberating progress; or, in the Marxist language, against the radical transformation of social relations under the effect of productive forces. For Benjamin, this optimistic dialectic was amply contradicted by the corrupting impulse that characterized the epoch.

In other words, Benjamin not only rejects the technician's

vision of historical progress and the freeing impact of productive relations, but moreover reverses this vision, by putting the question of the future at the center of his reflection. From this point of view, his thought marks a turning point because he breaks with the philosophies centered on convivance. In other words, the actual and the contemporary are reconfigured by the question of survival, which superbly ignores the social-democrat and positivist derivative of Marxism that Benjamin's *Theses on the Philosophy of History* attacks. By referring to Benjamin, I am not lauding a new utopian thought, but instead following his example in my own way by proceeding with a critique of the foundations of the contemporary political imaginary. My only ambition in the following pages is to analyze a rupture with the idea of a bright future and to give some consistency to a realistic vision of the political condition of human beings in our contemporary world.

1 The End of the Brilliance That the Future Will Bring

hen the American essayist Francis Fukuyama published *The End of History*, his text experienced immediate repercussions, well beyond the boundaries of his own country. What strikes us, in hindsight, is less the newness of the thoughts he was expressing—after all, Hegel had analogous ideas—but precisely the interest that the book and its provocative title fueled. The end of history: although many had the sense that the clock was still turning, something had broken at the end of the twentieth century. It was as if the vision of time that westerners shared and that they never stopped imposing on the rest of the world had become untenable. Until then, in fact, one bragged about being part of History. Whatever their disagreements, the Moderns shared the same appetite to transform the world, to go forward. No natural catastrophe, no horrible conflict that weakened the world during the last two centuries had eaten into this optimism, this faith in the powers of human reason, and in the resources of science and technology put into place by our fellow human beings. Man had progressed beyond monkey, and he had even managed to reach the moon. The end of the 1970s is in this respect distinctive. On earth, Southeast Asia was put to fire and sword, and sustained the ravages of American military technology, whereas the same great power managed to win its bet with the moon landing of three of its astronauts.

At the time, the criticism of U.S. imperialism was virulent. Nonetheless, American technical performance was unanimously applauded, as the sign of *progress* in human history, just like the discoveries in biology and the rapid developments of the computer industry, which appear as good news for a world insisting on its infatuation with *modernity*. I emphasize these two words, modernity and progress, because they constituted the leitmotifs for many generations, evoking the hope of a better world. In hindsight, it seems contradictory that the two great global conflicts of the last century, instead of tainting this hope, were able to fuel new expectations. Antagonistic ideologies found, in these conflicts, a favorable mold to develop and affront one another. In fact, modernity and progress only made sense when comforted by the idea that a human community—in this case, a state, a nation—had taken over its own destiny. Hence the preeminent role of the political as a materialization of this irreplaceable power of human beings to conduct their own affairs, to transform the world, giving themselves laws and collective goals.

The importance given to politics in this worldview is inseparable from Western humanism that emphasized the Promethean dimension of our societies. The civilized being, "industrious" as described by Enlightenment philosophers, came up with sufficient regulations to guarantee the possibility of carrying out his activity without hindrance. The first motive in the invention of civil duties, according to Hume, "is nothing but self-interest" (1992, 544). The formation of political power came within the framework of a more global dynamic aiming to promote a society of producers. The need for politics is the consequence of the individual's rise in power. The civil state constitutes the promise of a pacified world. Accepting certain constraints, whose intensity varies according to the regime in power, the individual enlarges his capacity to act. The political institution is the most efficient means to assure the safety of individual rights on his person and property, and to make order reign in the exchange relations of individuals. "But government extends farther its beneficial influence," writes Hume, "and not contented to protect men in those conventions they make for their mutual interest, it often obliges them to make such conventions, and forces them to seek their own advantage, by a concurrence in some common end or purpose" (1992, 538). This amounts to saying that in accepting the political state, men find themselves stimulated by their belonging to the group. The supreme cunning of the political consists in making private interest prevail at the exact moment when it seems to subject that interest to collective goals.

We would certainly say that Hume was a sly old fox, insensitive to the rhetoric of the free polis, which was so precious to philosophers since antiquity. It is true that, unlike Locke and Rousseau, he refuses to endorse the idea of an original social contract that would preside over the edification of "civil society." All this seems to him a pure and simple invention, and he prefers to hold onto a more pragmatic vision of things. Humans need politics to produce and reproduce; in addition, politics, under the displayed ideals of justice, has the advantage of promoting industry. Neither more nor less. This view of the public realm, as unromantic as it may be, seems to me to be very significant. In just a few lines, it draws the conditions of Enlightenment individualism. We knew that modernity rhymed with progress; but all of those who believed in development of science and more generally of productive forces must take political function seriously. Or, as Marx would say, no infrastructure without superstructure. For the establishment of a power and the struggles that start to harness this power are inseparable from the process of world transformation. Politics, science, and industry now form an indissoluble triangle.

This collusion between politics and modernity, and the way it frees itself in postrevolutionary bourgeois society from the religious sediment that enveloped it (even if the sacred remains present in certain aspects of republican sovereignty), could not be without consequences for the view of power that imposed itself progressively in Western democracies. This vision is realized through two key ideas. First of all, political activity is conceived as a vector of emancipation and its access becomes a true collective issue. Next, power as a center of decision must be able to remediate the imbalances created by progress. From liberal thinkers to Marx, the attempt has been made to find rationality in politics. There is an art of governance on which social peace and economic growth depend. It is about finding good measure, but this involves drawing the limits of action.

There is no surprise in the extraordinary abundance, in the eighteenth and nineteenth centuries, of treatises about the art of governance, as well as many reflections comparing the advantages and disadvantages of different political regimes. Through these texts, as in daily practice and power struggles, we perceive a real tension between what might be expected from the political realm. On the one hand, there is the hope that politics can somehow transcend itself, become a positive agent in the social dynamic, raising itself above particular interests and imposing a worldview that takes global evolutions into consideration. On the other hand, there is the more prosaic sentiment that politics remains stuck in sometimes sordid games that privilege the selfishness of the powerful.

Of course, in Europe during the entire nineteenth century, the state continually reinforced itself while simultaneously allowing criticism. It was in the name of progress that Marx pointed to the inadequacy of this political form, highlighting the way in which it sharpens social contradictions instead of helping to resolve them. At the same time, the bourgeois political power denounced by the author of *Capital* is a dynamic element in the system since it participates in the logic of accumulation that leads to the hegemony of one class over another. The state fully plays its part in the process that engenders a transnational capitalism harnessing human activity in even the most remote regions of the planet. Instrumentalized by the bourgeoisie, politics operates nevertheless with remarkable efficacy. According to Marx, it is there where the sword must be carried, and the revolution leads ineluctably to the conquest of the state apparatus by the working classes, with the instauration of a proletarian dictatorship. As we know, Marx's proclaimed objective was the decline of the state, which did not signify the end of politics, but its appropriation by all of society.

Without getting into a debate about the relevance of the Marxist viewpoint, we can observe Marx's fascination with politics, which he gives a special status in relation to other domains of social activity. As Miguel Abensour indicates, "Indeed, there is for Marx a sort of sublimity in the political realm. The exaltation is proper to the political sphere: in regard to other spheres, it is above and beyond" (Abensour 1997, 80). It is as if everything connected to the government were invested with a particular aura. There is no longer a true separation between religion and politics, which highlights the celestial metaphors that decorated Marx's first writings, and continued to do so later on. Marx's ambivalence is caused by his fascination for the sacredness of a domain that allows the individual to detach himself from his selfish interest in order to access the universal, and his hate for the manipulative reality of power. The state is the instrument par excellence of a certain power dynamic, of the violence that a minority exercises on the whole of society.

But, unlike Weber, whose view of the profound connection between power and violence fuels a pessimistic vision of politics, Marx sees the condition for emancipation in the political realm. History goes forward, propelled by modernization and industrial progress. Of course, the change, far from attenuating the forms of exploitation of man by man, exacerbates the contradictions between productive forces and relations of production. But it is precisely from the political struggle that the surmounting of such contradictions can come, along with the instauration of a new type of relations of humans among themselves and with nature. From this point of view, Marxism is characterized by unfailing optimism. Even the idea to construct a political organization of the masses, susceptible to overthrowing the powers in place and to carry out radical change, reflects the confidence which was never refuted in the positivism of political practice.

This confidence is largely based on the belief in the ephemeral character—on the scale of human history—of the institutions of power. "The state, then, has not existed from eternity. There have been societies that managed without it, that had no idea of the state and state authority" (Engels 1990 [1884], 272), which is similar to the idea that the day will come when we will have to file the state away in the "cabinet of Antiquities." This does not mean that politics will disappear but that they are susceptible to being embodied in new relations—Marx is vague on this point, evoking associative forms between producers. If we topple into utopia here, it is due to the fact that history never stops, and that it becomes necessary to imagine ourselves in the future, even if it means that we have to invent all sorts of preferentially reassuring possible futures. The eschatology of a classless society is the most spectacular expression of the religion of progress.

If we now consider the attitude of liberal thinkers toward

the state, it is easy to see the distance that separates them from the Marxist vision. They consider politics with distrust. They never stop complaining about the weight of the state. It is clear that one of their fundamental preoccupations involves the avoidance of any encroachment of the state onto the individual sphere. According to these thinkers, the best way to protect freedom is to avoid letting politics take the lion's share. Politics must be limited in its impact. Is that to say that sycophants of property and of the market have come to stigmatize the state? Things are far more complex, as Pierre Manent (1995 [1987]) has noted. On the one hand, the main worry of liberals is to avoid the hold of politics over civil society or over economic relations that are at the origin of wealth and whose central principle is private property. In this view, the preservation of individual liberty is the foundation of the social edifice. It matters that the people's sovereignty is practiced in a limited and relative manner. It is necessary, however, that the primacy accorded to individual freedom does not become synonymous with atomization. Benjamin Constant warns that "the danger of modern liberty is that, once absorbed in the joy of our private independence, we too easily renounce our right to share in political power" (1980, 509).

Civilization has experienced progress since antiquity, the economy prospers, and people are more connected: but does this mean that men must sacrifice the political dimension of freedom in favor of a purely selfish vision of their individual happiness? The public sphere would not be left to lie unsown: if they take it out on Rousseau, if they oppose any encroachment on civil society's sovereignty, liberals are completely aware that the state must take its part in the work of collective improvement. In fact, beginning with the French Revolution, the necessity to support institutional design and to enlarge the sphere of governance was part of a large consensus. Both Tocqueville and Marx are aware that this design is indispensable to resolve the social problems caused by the modern industrial economy. It shows how, in order to counter inequalities, "a *third party*, that of a central power whose mission is to symbolize, guarantee, and realize equality and resemblance" is constructed (Manent 1995 [1987], 107).

Driving itself toward a better future, society needs to be (well) governed. Technical and scientific progress is the condition of well-being. The world progresses in big leaps, and, in this dynamic, the place of politics, instead of being a problem, becomes crucial. We even find that the entrance into modernity is in line with the state's vampirization of all that was part of social ties and the practices of sociability. The establishment of systems of assistance entrusted to the public administration and which substituted for the forms of charitable protection illustrate this evolution. We are dealing with "the State's monopoly over instituting the social bond" (Gauchet 1997, 196). The figure of the welfare state that dominated the postwar period is without a doubt the most fully realized form of a certain relationship between the individual and the polis, devoted to redistribution. It implies that the individual participates actively in social solidarity, fulfilling her "social citizenship" (Rosanvallon 1998, 50). The history of the welfare state is marked by a growing mutualization of risks that makes the state the guarantor of social cohesion.

Until the 1980s, in Europe and the United States, welfare

was the paradigm of public action. During the *Trentes Glorieuses*, the thirty "glorious years" of economic prosperity in France, from 1945 through 1974, nothing could shake the confidence in the redistributive capacity of the state. In a country such as France, public opinion legitimated the state's control over the companies in charge of public services. At the time when the economy of "real" socialist countries was collapsing, France's Left took power, proposing a program of nationalizations. Never before in French history had state power attained such a degree. Banks, energy, and transportation were nationalized and politics exerted its control over the economy during a time when optimism was still the rule of the day. The French case is meaningful because it put change at the center of its preoccupations—the 1980s Socialist president François Mitterrand was not innovative in this sense: President Valéry Giscard d'Estaing, who governed from 1974 to 1981, already wanted to be the man of a new era. But the slogan of the moment, "change your life," was a hit. We expected politics, or at least society, to transform certain aspects of the world where we were living. The alternative seems, in hindsight, disarmingly simple: either reform or revolution, and nothing less. The disillusions were as high as the expectations. In a more and more difficult economic environment, the restructuring of industry and the exponential rise in unemployment pushed the state's impotence into the harsh light of day. At the end of the 1980s, more or less everywhere in the world, skepticism toward politics wreaked havoc, opening the world to populisms from unseen perspectives.

Without a doubt, this period marked the end of a cycle in the history of mentalities. Until then, the ideas of modernity and progress impressed themselves upon the world, carried by scientific and technical change. The philosopher Reinhart Koselleck (2004 [1979]) has highlighted how much the modern apprehension of time is based on the permanent tension between expectation and experience, inseparable from the notion of progress. Analyzing the evolution of the thinking about time since the Middle Ages, he shows in particular how the birth of the modern state was accompanied by what he calls a "secularization of time": up until the middle of the sixteenth century, the representation of time included the future and, in this particular case, the end of time. The Church's history took into consideration the possible end of the world, and the notion of salvation played a primordial role in it.

Salvation is the horizon of expectation in the perspective within which the history of the Church develops. In this representation of time, it is clear that the future is integrated with time, playing an essential role in making the Roman Church's sovereignty durable. We are at the antipodes of linear time, since the end of the world is in some way registered in the immediate experience of the present and the past. The rupture of modern times is produced with the emergence of human history, disconnected from the expectation of the end of the world. If the Germanic Holy Roman Empire is part of an eschatology that defines its role and gives it legitimacy, the modern state then appears disconnected from religious history and capable of subduing religious factions. In this context, the prophetic function was given a pounding. The conception of the world that came from certitude in the last judgment was finished, even if this conception was once essential in the establishment of action principles.

At this moment, we enter a world where the future is thought of in terms of probability, and prophecy makes way for calculations and strategies. We are focused on calculating the probability of events liable to arrive or not: prognostics substitutes for prophecy. We move from a static temporal structure characterized by the cyclical nature of history to a dynamic structure where the acceleration and irreversibility of time reign. The future becomes a synonym for the unknown. The fact that this future is based on us and our own actions implies that the practitioners of politics adopt a very different attitude regarding courses of action marked by eschatological expectations. The flight of time is caught thanks to the science of prognostication, which has become an indispensable instrument to act on a political situation. This science incorporates the three dimensions of time in its calculation. In order to control the present, it is necessary to be able to anticipate the future, grounding the analysis on the lessons of the past.

Koselleck has shown how the temporal rendering of history has been transformed in modern times. He analyzes this mutation by introducing the concepts of experience fields and the horizon of expectation. The biggest innovation at the end of the seventeenth century was the dissociation between expectation and experience. Since then, "not only did the gap between past and future become greater, but also the difference between experience and expectation had to be constantly and ever more rapidly bridged to enable one to live and act" (2004 [1979], 270). The interest of Koselleck's approach lies in his concern with problematizing the representation of the relation between present and future that dominated the modern era.

Today, however, the situation is quite different: the conception that he analyzes, dominated by the idea of progress, made way in the political field for a configuration of practices and discourse that draws a horizon of incertitude. The aim of progress put itself in the tension between present and future, working to overcome the gap between experience and expectation. In this way the "concepts of expectation" were constructed in order to anticipate the future movement of history. Republicanism, socialism, and all the other "isms" that we find in political discourse, as well as at the heart of social science, participate in this venture. "Modernity is movement plus uncertainty," writes Georges Balandier (1988, 161) associating this temporal regime with the idea of change and openness toward the future. On the contrary, it is precisely the idea of the future that is a problem today. Is it still possible to have expectation, in the sense that Koselleck understands it? For him, the formula of modernity that he summarizes as "the leaner the experience, the grander the expectation" would have to now make way for a completely different relationship to the future, namely, "the grander the experience, the more cautious but also the more open is the expectation" (1979, 326–27).

It is not certain that expectation is as the German philosopher describes. Don't we have to deal with a true crisis of the future?[1] The twentieth century was the crucible of ideologies that subordinated the present to the future, haunted by the crazy project of constructing a "new man." First the idea of progress was confronted with hard reality, while the world became aware of the havoc that could result from technological progress. That such advancement might be put into use to carry out a massive extermination of one part of humanity during the Second World War; that the most sophisticated science could be at the origin of an atomic weapon and would make the ghost of pure and simple destruction of human life weigh on the future—there was everything one needed to nourish all the disenchantment regarding the "brilliance that the future would bring."

As long as it dealt with a military risk—in other words, that it was part of the strategies of states—we could imagine that a real political control of danger was possible. After all, one of the lessons of the Cold War was that the antagonistic powers only used the dissuasive power of fatal weapons. Nevertheless, Hiroshima opened a new chapter in the history of mentalities. Paradoxically, the extraordinary scientific and technical performance that represented the discovery of nuclear fission and the adjustment of its different applications also announced the end of progress ideologies. We fully entered *the risk era*. This movement was amplified in the last third of the twentieth century when people became aware that economic and population growth would not continue forever.

1. I borrow this expression from K. Pomyan (1980).

The petroleum crisis of 1973 provoked for the first time a collective representation of the limits of the planet's energy potential. The awareness that progress could eventually dry up resources made it seem like a danger to humanity. This view of things was further intensified by a certain number of accidents linked to technology: industrial accidents such as the one in Seveso in 1976 and most of all the catastrophe of Chernobyl in 1986.

Is confidence in the future thus finished? More profoundly, the crisis of the future becomes a mirror for the present. As François Hartog observes, "The present has spread itself as much in the direction of the future as in that of the past" (2003, 216; see also Taguieff 2000). This disposition translates in part to the importance given to risks and their anticipation, and in part to the inflation of the devices of patrimonialization and commemoration. In this configuration, it is clear that the future is above all conceived of as the asylum of all uncertainties. It simultaneously disconcerts and disquiets. In the past, we hoped to join in the network of rational prognoses; hence the echo that the idea of prospective experienced in the 1960s. Granted, we already began to worry about the damages of growth, but, instead of renouncing the project, the prospect and its implementation in state planning was part of optimistic voluntarism. It would be a mistake to identify planning only with triumphant communism. Let's not forget that this idea was part of the intellectual arsenal of the directors of developed capitalism. This is how Jean Monnet, before acting as the bearer of the European ideal and whom no one could suspect of having socialist leanings, became the manager of the Commissariat au Plan created in France following the war. In this capacity, Monnet surrounded himself with the most innovative economists of the coming generation.

Programmer, planner: these activities took on their full meaning in the perspective of an open future, from the stimulation that "expectation" represented. European construction as Jean Monnet initiated it came out of a mental attitude that advocated hope while leaning against more concrete experience. The masterpiece in the subject is the strategy that founds Europe on the necessity of a common market. In this strategy, we are in full economic rationality since it is based on a well-understood relationship between costs and advantages in a domain of limited action, but within which the public can directly measure its positive impact. The prospective vision of the world from which Europe came seems inapt in relation to the "presentism" that prevails today. Everything occurs as if, contrary to the prospective attitude that glorified voluntarism and rationality, the postmodern polis preferred to absorb itself in the fascination of the immediate—the object par excellence of the society of spectacle—or to stay away from the future in this inflation of memory shown by the extraordinary blossoming of symbols and museums.

Should we be surprised that the entrance into the risk era translates into a complete remaking of our relationship to history and the emergence of a new temporal regime? Anthropologists have shown how societies spatially far from our own have developed a completely different relationship to time. By distinguishing "cold societies" and "hot societies,"

Lévi-Strauss invites us to consider the existence of different types of historicity. He specifies that this distinction "does not propose a difference in the nature of societies, does not place societies in separate categories, but refers to the subjective attitudes that societies adopt vis-à-vis history and in the variable manners in which they conceive of it" (1998, 568:67). Some societies see "disorder and threat" in history, while others use history as an instrument "to act on the present and transform it" (Lévi-Strauss 1983, 1218). Western civilization adopted the latter point of view, which led it to stigmatize as "primitive" the societies that did not share this perspective. The same ethnocentrism provoked westerners to oppose the cumulative character of these societies' relationship to history to the irreducible inertia of the savage mind, closed to the future and incapable of transforming itself.

This confidence in modernity seems almost like an anachronism today, to the extent that Lévi-Strauss, writing many years later about the opposition between hot and cold societies, observes not without humor: "I asked myself if, at this fin de siècle, our own societies were not showing perceptible signs of cooling." In their own way in a different context, they would try to "oppose the current of history and suspend time" (1998, 598:66–69). It is as if the presentism that marks our era were a possible strategy when confronted with the movement of history: a strategy that seems like the surest way to stop time from continuing its forward march. How can we interpret this cognitive attitude? It could have something in common with superstition: confronted with the premonition of coming danger, we would practice the politics of the ostrich and bury our head in the sand by refusing to confront the future directly and absorbing ourselves in the sound and fury of the present. Unless—using an alternative strategy— we try to tame the future by elaborating new principles of action. It is in this context that the precautionary principle intruded and we will see the debates that its usage stirs up. "To act in an uncertain world": this is the catchphrase of the new generation of experts and politicians. Some will go as far as lauding an "enlightened catastrophism" (see Dupuy 2002). The approach is significant: it goes against all the impulses of the last century. No more hope, no more utopia: we are stuck in a present of a world without a future.

But what present is this about? For the theorists of postmodernism, the fragmentation of the present and the disintegration of the order of time characterize the current era. The absence of continuity and the incapacity to unify the past, present, and future causes this fascination for artistic experiments that play with devices such as collage and montage to express the ephemeral, the discontinuous, and the chaotic. Postmodernism is inseparable from the challenging of totalizing metadiscourses, and it privileges plays on words, finding its model in Derridean deconstruction. According to Fredric Jameson, one of the most visible intellectual figures of postmodernism, it is not "a style, but more a cultural dominant" (1984, 53–92). It presents itself, in reaction to modernism and its avant-gardes (Picasso, Joyce, and others), not as the source of novelty, but as the deconstruction of expression. Parody and pastiche are at the heart of a game in which the present annexes the past, where we pretend to copy masterpieces by turning around their meaning, where we reify, where we instrumentalize cultural products without worrying about moving forward. Postmodernism is, in a sense, the end of history. Or, rather, the triumph of historicism. Jameson understands historicism as the opposite of a return to the past. He sees it as a proliferation of references, not of the past but of our representations of the past, such as these "retro" films that stage our representations of the past, or the architectural ensembles such as the Bonaventura Hotel, constructed by John Portman in Los Angeles.

From the point of view that interests us, that of history and of time, postmodernism questions the essence of the temporal sequence: present, past, future. Without explicitly evoking the end of history, this is more about a back-and-forth between past and present. But there is no position whatsoever on the horizon of the future. Even the notion of "post" brings into question the entire idea of a single sense of time. We are thousands of light-years from the idea of the perfection possibility (Rousseau) which was coterminous with the representations of modernity. Postmodernism corresponds to the *mise en spectacle* of the collapse of progress's regulating idea that long oriented social behavior and relationships. Does the triumph of postmodernism translate as the prodigious expansion of capital on the global scale, as Jameson suggests? In any case, we are experiencing the imposition of a figure of time in which the future is no longer identified with progress, and within which operates an incessant *mise en abyme* of the present.

2 Globalization and the State: A False Debate?

The dearth of the future at the base of the postmodernist discourse comes from a more profound phenomenon that affects our perception of the world. We could point to the dialectic of closing and opening linked to the experience of globalization—an opening because the new planetary situation is characterized by the intensity of circulation phenomena, and by the scope of human, capital, and information fluxes. Accepted by society, globalization seems to promise the construction of a boundless world. At the same time, it corresponds to an awareness of the shrinking of space and time. The globalized economy is an "economy with the capacity to work as a unit in real time, or in chosen time, on a planetary scale" (Castells 2001 [1996], 136). This situation exacerbates the consciousness of a world closed in on itself, a compacted universe. Postmodernity is thus defined as a phenomenon of "the compression of time and space" (Harvey 1990, 240). It is precisely this awesome intensification of flux, along with the ease with which one can circulate from one end of the planet to the other and the possibility of transmitting information to the most remote places that aggravates this sentiment of closing and loss of horizon.

We are accustomed to emphasizing the economic aspects of globalization. It is true that globalization corresponds to a displacement from a primarily industry-based economy to one where activities of conception play a major role and where trade growth is tied to financial deregulation, which implies new approaches in terms of the circulation of capital. Perhaps we have given insufficient weight to the fact that globalization is first and foremost a cultural phenomenon. As the economist Daniel Cohen observes, "Globalization makes people see a world that shatters their expectations; the tragedy is that it reveals itself as utterly incapable of satisfying them" (2004, 16). If this last observation deserves some attention, let us retain the idea that globalization manifests itself in the apprehension of a new landscape. The Amazonian Indians quickly understood that the destruction of the forest corresponded to the needs of transnational firms, and was only the concretization in the field of a logic that placed them in the world economy. At the same time, they discovered technologies they would never have imagined, neither their existence nor their purpose.

The violence of globalization must not be purely and simply seen as a process of domination or as a renewed form of colonialism. Its impact is all the greater because of the profound change in our awareness of time and space that globalization entails, as Robertson notes: "Globalization as a concept refers both to the compression of the world and the intensification of our consciousness of the world as a whole"

(Robertson 1992, 8). For westerners, the fear of a closed-off world expresses itself through a strong feeling of insecurity. A sector of the economy needs only to show signs of weakness to provoke the possibility of relocating to another country. In the confrontations between employees and employers that have always punctuated economic life, the outcome used to be a solution that took social conditions and local economies into account. Now, we "think globally," meaning that reloca-tion appears from the outset to be a meaningful alternative. In the face of possible relocation, workers have a dilemma: either they accept the "sacrifices," or the company simply disappears. Above and beyond this recurrent blackmail, the thing that weakens people the most is the perception of the extraordinary closeness of *other* lands, whether in eastern Europe, Asia, or elsewhere. There is also a feeling of tem-poral proximity: in a few weeks, or even a few days, one can create an analogue company on the other side of the world.

In practice the compression of time and space can be perceived as a threat, not only because it accentuates the pressure of the invisible hand in the form of the omnipotent market, but also insofar as it enables a violent intrusion of otherness into our world. This was the case on September 11, 2001, where a place that represented the quintessence of the market was brutally attacked by a group that incarnated radi-cal exteriority. We realized how easy it was for people that we tended to think of as being on the other side of the world to reach the heart of the system by transforming peaceful tech-nologies into fatal weapons. We often say that 9/11 marked a turning point, because it revealed both the limits of hyperpowerfulness and the determination of Islamic fundamentalists. The fact that America became vulnerable stunned imaginations, and many already saw the looming threat of a targeted nuclear strike against metropolises in the United States. More profoundly perhaps, what most disturbs the civilized and reasonable human being in each of us is the possibility that an attack could happen at any moment "in our own backyards," whereas during the Cold War we became accustomed to a delocalization of conflicts. The Middle East, Afghanistan, Africa: these people were tearing each other's guts out at a respectable distance from where we lived.

The awareness of globalization cannot, therefore, be summarized by recognition of the increasing interdependence of economies. It lies as much—if not more—in the interiorization of a simple and distressing fact by the citizens of developed countries: namely, that they will never again be "sheltered" from the threats of distant places. Such places were hitherto confined to the margins, whereas today they are capable of organizing themselves in very "modern" ways and bursting into the center. The discourse of modernity, conversely, was articulated around the idea of an irreducible difference between all that represents civilization and fits into the scheme of progress, and these Others who, while belonging to humanity, were nonetheless destined to the inertia of beings without history. We are now part of the same planet and our fates are increasingly interwoven. The possibility for optimism remains: we can still delight in the compression of globalization that breaks down certain barriers between societies, reverses prejudices, and obliges cultural mixing. Métissage and hybridization became the way to characterize the long-awaited possibility of a meeting between cultures which had been separated and isolated by prevailing ideologies. The opposite of this ecumenical vision is an interpretation that highlights the virulence of the tensions generated by another huge present-day reality: the other side of world unity is that resources and riches have to be shared.

Twenty or so years ago, we wanted to do away with all form of segregation. All French people recall the great commemoration of the French Revolution and the multicultural parade organized by Jean-Paul Goude. This was the great reconciliation—the melting pot. It was under the aegis of the whites, of course. The Other was present, but we had the upper hand and had summoned him to help us hold our own history up to the mirror of this commemoration. We all knew that as soon as the celebrations were over everyone would go back to his place, with us in the center and them on the periphery, according to an order which, at the time, seemed inviolable. At that period, an open world meant that distance was not about to disappear. Even those who criticized the new incarnations of colonialism and Western domination placed the opposition between center and periphery at the heart of their ideas and spoke of conditions for a better future. It is precisely the reach of this model that now seems problematic, for at least two reasons. The first relates to the pressure that poverty and otherness exert directly. On the one hand, we are no longer dealing with the category of "the Third World" passively suffering the consequences of the capitalist dynamic. Instead, we now have an increasingly diverse group of societies, including countries which compete in the world economy and voraciously hold onto their share of market. The second reason for the weakening of the center/periphery paradigm is related to the displacement going on with these categories. It is clear today that the periphery has become an integral part of the center, as the struggles of "illegal immigrants" eloquently demonstrate: exclusion is at the heart of our societies (see also Das and Poole 2004).

In this context, the main problem our societies have to confront becomes clearer. Although many questions may arise concerning their future, the question that has to be addressed today seems to me to be the political question. We must deal with "acting together," to use a term from Hannah Arendt (1968), and instituting the means through which acting together can appropriately reflect society's demands. What expression can citizens' questionings find, and in what framework? What does governing mean in this context of global compression? If we refer to the last era, we can see that it was dominated by the social question. It acted — we saw it — to ensure the conditions of the reproduction of the dominant economic regimes, in Communist as well as in capitalist countries, by constructing adapted regulations. On the capitalist side, equilibrium seemed to be reached with the model of the welfare state and its variations in Western countries. This organization was the nice part of politics; it delegated the capacity to make social justice prevail and restricted the abuses of a market economy. On the Communist side, the state held the whole of economic as well as social responsibilities.

The intensity of the social question led on the one hand to a considerable reinforcement of the impact of politics by widening its scope of legitimate intervention—traditionally limited to the field of the police force, diplomacy, and defense—and secondly by shaping the demand for politics in our societies. And yet what do we see, when the end of the twentieth century is simultaneously marked by the collapse of communism and the financialization of the economy and its worldwide deregulation? The parameters of global trade are progressively coming to impose their rules, and the state appears increasingly eclipsed in terms of determining factors over which it no longer has any real leverage. Bearing witness to this trend is the reaction of French prime minister Lionel Jospin when questioned in connection with the suppression of 7,500 jobs in Europe by an important French company: "One should not expect everything from the state and the government," he said (France 2, September 3, 1999). We can see, in that case, the recognition of the limits of political action. It is all the more symptomatic of a general trend because it comes not from a free-marketing advocate but from a Socialist leader. Another striking thing about this speech is the absence of perspective. The statesman wants to be realistic, so he refers to the impotence of the public realm. Politics seems to be stripped of its capacity of projection. This is the opposite of the vision that had prevailed during the Thirty Glorious years, when politics was made to forecast and program. It's as if its role were reduced to that of accompanying, as far as possible, the general disillusionment, and of absorbing, at least in words, the jolts of the global economy.

This design is the result of the swing already announced by a regime of historicity with no opening toward the future.

In these conditions, it is not surprising that belief in the impact of politics has given way to skepticism. This is all the more the case because everyone senses that the changes in the global economy will not strengthen the nation-state form, which had, in the last century, a structuring role as far as politics was concerned. The decline in the state's sovereignty over the economy is related to the capacity of world business to operate within the framework of market-governed regulation that partially escapes state influence. Consequently, governments no longer control markets—in fact, even the opposite is happening (Strange 1996). Indeed, economic policies depend mostly on an economic and financial situation that is hard to control at the national level. In addition, post-bipolar evolution is leading to a destruction of the sacred aura surrounding sovereignties. At the same time, the rising power of "global cities"—those metropolises of transnational capitalism that "concentrate a disproportionate share of corporate power and are one of the key sites for its valorization," but which "also concentrate a disproportionate share of the disadvantaged and are one of the key sites for their devalorization" (Sassen 1998, xxxiv)—also contributes to a limiting of the impact of traditional state systems. Not only weakened by the triumph of the market economy, state sovereignty is also challenged by the forming of large groupings integrating entire regions of the globe: the European Union, MERCOSUR and NAFTA, and ASEAN and APEC in Asia. The state is also overwhelmed by the complexity of the challenges and caught between the demands of the global and the tenacious realities of the local.

We have significantly glossed over many of the political consequences of globalization. Doesn't the interdependence between economies, as well as the need to change the scale in the management of financial and human flows, have a long term consequence of weakening that concept so precious to politicians—sovereignty? Of course, there are still borders and delimitations which make it possible to distinguish the nation-states that constitute them. In the same way, as current world conflicts illustrate, the claim of the full exercise of sovereignty remains omnipresent just about everywhere. But the politics of the great powers, which reached its peak with the Cold War and was expressed in a veritable world order focused around the East-West divide, is giving way to a more complex reality, marked by a double process. On the one hand, there is the apparent hegemony of the superpower, the United States. On the other hand, there is a sense of the weakness of this organized power in the face of violence—of which September 11 was the most spectacular manifestation. As Bertrand Badie observes, "The fragmentation and the dissemination of international violence that has become more social than political, disorients canons and makes the dreams of anti-missile missiles absurd" (2004, 278).

One of the most visible effects of globalization is an exacerbation of inequalities, notably between North and South, and a breakdown of the traditional social and cultural fabrics. In this context, the appearance of new kinds of violence based on self-sacrifice that can take more or less sophisticated shapes changed the classic model of war studies. Confronted with state violence, the action of deterritorialized, mobile, and fragmented networks now tends to prevail. These developments are enough to destabilize the widespread strategies involving a central organization that leaned heavily on the performance of the armament industry.

What is foretold, to borrow the expression of Bertrand Badie (2004), is thus "the impotence of power." Contemporary international relations have entered, he tells us, a new era. In other words, the existence of a globalized stage where the flow of terrorist movements is as intense as the flow of information (the latter multiplying the former) profoundly transforms our perception of power—based as it is on the primacy of the nation-state. Perhaps it is time to realize the obsolete nature of a system of government that proved itself throughout the last century. The nation-state, based on the isomorphism between people, territory, and legitimate sovereignty, is profoundly called into question by globalization. The proliferation of deterritorialized groups and the "diasporic diversity" that we see almost everywhere have the effect of creating new, translocal solidarities. We see identity constructions emerging that go beyond the national framework. In their own way, state policies play a part in fostering this situation by giving rise to migratory movements. The anthropologist Arjun Appadurai (1996) has underlined the highly heterogeneous nature of such movements. Refugees, workers, specialists from companies or international organizations, and tourists are very different types of migrants. But, in every case, widespread movement is at the root of new, subjective referents that are making forms of identification linked to territory and the state increasingly anachronistic. Refugees, tourists, students, workers, and migrants all form, in their way, a delocalized "transnation."

Under these conditions—and it is the extreme consequence to which the observations of Appadurai lead—it would seem that we have entered the postnational era. The new forms of organization playing a prime political role, in areas as diverse as the environment, the economy, and humanitarian aid, show a fluidity and flexibility that contrasts with the rigid structures of traditional state apparatuses. The nongovern- mental organizations (NGOs) being developed all around the world, often in connection with crisis situations, are highly representative of a new political model more directly anchored in civil society, one that blithely transcends national borders. The transnationality that increasingly characterizes the globalized world requires new networks of solidarity and more labile modes of action. Postnational sovereignties are already emerging (see Pandolfi 2002). Even the idea of patriotism still has some value, inasmuch as we are dealing with "mobile, plural and contextual" patriotism.

Appadurai joined the ranks of the political scientist James Rosenau, for whom the state no longer plays a central role in a world that puts a premium on "governance without government" (Rosenau and Czempiel 1992). This governance involves not only the political dimension, but also other players from civil society. In a world increasingly threatened by various kinds of turbulence (Rosenau 1990)—including terrorism, the proliferation of nuclear weapons, and mafia-orchestrated trafficking—the need for transnational governance is gradually becoming obvious. The increasing power of organizations aiming to provide types of regulation on a larger scale is the symptom of an evolution that leads Badie (1999) to raise the question of a "world without sovereignty."

Those who see in the erosion of the state one of the highlights of the new international order are quick to affirm that we have entered the "glocal" era. Are we moving toward extended world governance understood as the implementing of common rules by an authority whose legitimacy is recognized on a global scale? Analysts highlight the new power that supranational organizations have acquired, as well as the appearance of "nongovernmental" organizations which have succeeded in occupying center stage in contexts where the only authority was hitherto held by the diplomacy of states. Furthermore, the recrudescence of ethnic conflicts destabilizes the state. We can recognize, along with Badie, that "the state must compose itself with a renewed volatility of identity, cooperate with nonofficial international actors, . . . adhere to a world space that is structured according to several modes and which obeys multiple temporalities" (Badie 1995, 106).

But is it necessary to go further and decipher the first steps of true global governance? On the contrary, wouldn't we be victims of an illusion? Would globalization simply feed the illusions of those who believe in the inescapable decline of nation-states? It is this last position that Samy Cohen supports when he maintains that, far from becoming weaker, state political formations adapt perfectly to globalization. He argues that "the decadence of the state is mainly responsible for the plagues such as the Mafia, drug trafficking, and clandestine immigration" (2003, 39). In the same way, national sovereignties remain the principal actors in the fight against terrorism.

One will certainly oppose to this vision the fact that the states consented, within the framework of European construction, to give up a share of their sovereignty and to accept the prospect of integration in a broader unit. One will also call upon the growing influence that nonofficial and transnational organizations such as NGOs have on the global scene. For Cohen, however, the concessions made by the states in the European context is part of a pragmatic program which enables them to preserve, or even reinforce, their power. In addition, without denying the increased role of civil society, its action is only effective within the framework narrowly defined by the play of nation-states.

We might as well say that the real protagonists of the international scene are indeed state sovereignties, beginning with the United States, and that the space of initiative that transnational and nongovernmental organizations profit from is severely limited by the involved states. Confronted with the supporters of a world without sovereignty and governance without government, Cohen shows that national interest is a very contemporary idea, and that it is rather by the excess of sovereignty that international relations go wrong. Many things oppose those political scientists who demand that we take seriously the consequences of globalization on the political level to those who, on the contrary, see in globalization only a misadventure that could not profoundly modify the system of international relations. Is it possible to get out of this dilemma? In order to consider globalization, must we throw out the baby—in this case, state sovereignty—with the bathwater? Or must we, on the contrary, champion the resistance of the state with the risk of minimizing the innovation of the globalization process?

We can also bypass this debate and try to consider modernity with the hindsight of the historian. It is the position that Jean-François Bayart (2004) adopts, and for whom globalization should not be regarded as a radical innovation. In the nineteenth century we already witnessed what he calls "global political experiments," from the Napoleonic wars to the colonial experiment and the rise of imperialism. This first globalization resulted in the appearance of international organizations in the economic and financial fields, but also in the political and associative domains. The global expansion of governance continued with the formation of the state, maintains Bayart, who insists on the fact that, far from being incompatible, globalization and sovereignty can mutually reinforce one another. This demonstration would equally apply to the current era, in that increasing integration of the international system can cause a "logic of identity retraction," such as when the reaffirmation of their adherence to the European Union reinforced national belonging in central and eastern European countries. "The transnational dimension of the international system is the substance of the state" (Bayart 2004, 127): this somewhat provocative formula summarizes the prospect that historical sociology proposes by highlighting the compatibility between the changes of capitalism and the persistence of the national referent. Globalization may be far from transforming international politics, and in fact it may prove to be favorable to the emergence and the reinforcement of states, to what Bayart calls the "crystallization of a system of states" (2004, 130).

If I bring up this discussion between specialists in international relations, it is not only for its intrinsic interest. The fact that the question of the role and even the future of the nation-state is posed today is revealing of the penetrating doubt regarding the relevance of what used to constitute the exercise of power in our societies. It is as if, ultimately, the central question was that of the future of state sovereignty in the dubious world where we live. This kind of interrogation has an obvious advantage: it obliges us to take seriously the outcomes of an evolution that the sometimes naive enthusiasm of *global studies* tends to occult. At the same time, the discussion is revealing of a debate polarized by the question of the state.

Hence the propensity to put the problem in institutional terms, as if the essential question was that of organizational form and the involution which might affect it in the current era. Perhaps, more profoundly, the force behind this political debate is a confused intuition that was somehow displaced into our understanding of the political. The type of political organization, however, is not what is really being challenged. The target is more a certain concept of sovereignty that was the heart of the system, both in its national dimension and its global articulation. In the same way, it is not important for the time being to wonder whether globalization caused this displacement, or if it is only its revealer.

As I see it, the central point is this political displacement, which may end up reorganizing the institutional arena but is by no means confined to it. We must try to identify the "stuff" of this displacement. We must also avoid falling back on old moralizing or psychologizing ideas about political disillusionment. I will highlight what is constructed in this displacement process, in terms of practices and political representations. With this intention, the anthropological perspective opens the broader question of the human relationship to power, by offering the terms of comparison too often ignored or suppressed by the discourse of modernity. Nevertheless, it is not a question of a rather arbitrary gesture which would consist in substituting one point of view for another, with the "regard" of the anthropologist considered more penetrating than a different specialist's perspective. It is quite simply the nature of displacement, and the stakes which it draws, that encourages one to take this track. We are dealing with processes whose range far exceeds the dialectic within which we sought to confine them. What is happening today has only little to do with the institutional and conceptual frameworks that we are used to. From the anthropologist's perspective, this situation is not particularly shocking. After all, it is one of anthropology's contributions to have highlighted the political devices that did not tally with the philosophical and political concepts to which we were accustomed.

3 Virtual Europe, a Space of Uncertainty

We are already experiencing the dislocation of politics, for our destiny is now inseparable from the construction of the European Union (EU). We are more or less aware that the nation, the fatherland — everything that our citizenship rests on — is now part of a broader entity. The future of the European Union weighs strongly on our political psyche. This Europe creates stress, as can be observed from the vote on the 2005 referendum of the European constitution. The EU project was first presented as the search for a politico-institutional formula capable of efficiently achieving integration and unification. At first, it seemed like a response to a broader requirement — namely, that of reinforcing economic stability in Europe in order to assert its power in the international market, on a par with the United States and the Asian giants, in a situation where the globalization of exchange and the existence of multinational corporations made the national scale too narrow. We realize, however, that this construction that began with the highest rationality, remains, fifty years after its creation, a factor of disorder and uncertainty.

Looking retrospectively at the great stages of European construction, two seemingly contradictory interpretations are possible. On the one hand, we can stress the continuity of a process which in forty years made the exchange between member states possible, set up a powerful political instrument and a consistent institutional framework, as well as a number of common policies. The Schuman plan and the creation of the European Coal and Steel Community (ECSC), the treaties of Rome, the first election of the European Parliament by universal suffrage, the signature of the Single European Act, the Maastricht treaty, the creation of a large European market, the birth of the single currency — these events and milestones have distinguished the long-term project that profoundly changes the geopolitics of the European continent. This reading of the last half century would satisfy the pioneers of the Community. Don't the facts thus spectacularly refute all the forms of skepticism that opposed the construction of the EU?

And yet, one could offer a different version of the EU's history — one that would highlight the multiple crises that have marred European construction. This process, we would say, has had problems and met obstacles. It is a euphemism. In reality, the Community project has never stopped feeding dissensions and causing dispute, both between the countries and within each of them. Even the process of European construction was punctuated by important discontinuities. In nearly one half century, Europe experienced just as many idle periods as strong times.

The history of the Community is a two-speed history.

There is the express lane; that is, the imperturbable implementation of the founding project. There are also all the missteps and delays which fed mistrust and irony with regard to a project so often returned to the drawing board. To be European today is both an obvious fact—it is enough to belong to the one of the member states—and a consistently postponed deadline. The political union is still far from being achieved, and the status of the European citizen is only sketchily outlined in the texts. Whatever its effective rationality, the European project has always been difficult to assimilate because it has never unfurled itself in our present.

European Community time has several dimensions. To begin with, it wants to *anticipate* and thus projects us into a remote future. It also acts in *continuous creation*: backward movement causes renewal, and history becomes a perpetual beginning. Lastly, Community time is the obsession of the calendar, the *urgency* established in theory. There is a major difficulty for the citizen who justifiably wonders what one means by Europe, so much so that these three dimensions are tangled up in one another. Let us try to distinguish them from each other.

Early on, Europe was placed under the sign of irreversibility. It was presented by its promoters as offering the only chance to reconcile France and Germany, and more generally to preserve peace and prosperity between nations which had just come out of a world war. If the ECSC Treaty of 1951 lays down a limited objective, since it relates to the production and distribution of coal and steel, its preamble is nonetheless explicit: it is a question "of founding, by the establishment of an economic community, the first steps of a broader and more profound community between people long-opposed by bloody divisions." In other words, far from being an end in itself, economic co-operation was to be the instrument of a broader ambition. Robert Schuman clearly stated a similar objective in his historical declaration of May 9, 1950: "This proposal will lead to the realisation of the first concrete foundation of a European federation indispensable to the preservation of peace" (Schuman 1950).

The idea of the founders of Europe (including Jean Monnet, Robert Schuman, Konrad Adenauer, and Paul-Henri Spaak) was that a transnational unity be created to focus on specific areas, beginning with an open market for the European Coal and Steel Community (ECSC). They imagined that once the European member states cooperated in these areas, the interdependence of policy would promote the "spillover effect" into others. The aim of the Monnet method was to initiate "engrenage," an "action trap" in which once the agents are set in a specific course of action, they find themselves obliged to take further actions which point them in a direction that they did not necessarily intend to take. As a result, the "engrenage" functioned in such a way that it would be impossible for the member states to step back. They are more and more involved in the whole process, even though no great formal proclamation on federalism has been announced.

"Europe will not be made all at once, or according to a single plan. It will be built through concrete achievements which first create a *de facto* solidarity," declared Robert

Schuman (1950). When he comments on this text in his memoirs, Jean Monnet writes: "It was the fundamental choice of a method to continually integrate objects and spirits" (1976, 434). Since European construction is conceived through the notion of "engrenage," the interest of a proposal is measured by its capacity to further engage the implicated countries.

This is also how Jacques Delors reasons later, when he explores the possibilities of European revival. At that moment, the project has three possible avenues: advancement in the institutional field, a monetary union, or a large European market. The new president of the Commission chooses the large market: it is the least original option, but it fits fully into "engrenage," extending the field of concrete achievements in order to further solidarity. The Single European Act will carry out this program by narrowly binding the economies of the member states. The method, faithful to the inspiration of the founding fathers, privileges economic provisions. Once again, the question of a political Europe fails to be posited directly. It is simply a question of taking the steps of harmonization that are essential to the opening of the Large European market. By privileging economic integration, Europe continues its forward march in the name of a rationality that can be summarized in these terms: confronted by the United States and Asia, Europe must give itself the means to become a full-fledged world power.

In the 1950s, it was the need to definitively standardize Franco-German relations that formed the central argument; thirty years later, what mattered was Europe's place in economic competition. Once this global objective was put into place, the approach consisted of installing the required technical and legal apparatuses. This is where the idea of European construction, understood as a transparent process, becomes effective. Indeed, each advance in a particular field (agriculture, environment, etc.) implies a series of maneuvers in the name of harmonization; however, it quickly becomes clear that these maneuvers demand further steps in order to obtain the optimal performance of the European market, and so on. Political scientists call this mechanism "the spillover effect" (Haas 1958; Keohane and Hoffmann 1991). The spillover dynamics accounted for the implementation of directives and rules which could never have been imposed separately by the member states' governments. As Jean Monnet understood from the beginning, it was necessary to find the means of *involving* and *interlocking* the member states. This occurred in a double objective: initially, to oblige them to go further in the process of integration; then to make it almost impossible to reject a directive without excluding oneself from European construction.

The stages reached since the Schuman plan affirm that the vision of the pioneers was lucid: creating a mechanics founded on law and economy was the surest means of binding European countries together. They stood to profit not only from the Common Market, but also from certain policies, as was the case for France with the common agricultural policy. But the experiment proved how difficult it was to escape the spillover effect. Economic integration finds a correlate in the juridical plan: the creation of Community legislation distinct from international law, as well as the existence of a

European Court of Justice applying to both states and individuals, marks an innovation. On the institutional level, the "triangle" formed by the Council, the Commission, and the Parliament constitutes an original plan. The monopoly of initiative is allocated not to the governments but to the Commission, whose proposals can only be amended by the unanimity of member states. The erection of an autonomous third party in relation to the states is the element that ensures the community operation of the system. While the Council is in charge of decision making, the power of proposal making—and therefore the capacity for innovation—necessarily comes from the Commission, which also crafted the domestic market in the form of common currency—the Euro. The system represents, according to the formula of former European commissioner Pascal Lamy, "a technological jump of governance" (2004, 38). It still remains, as Lamy observes, that "the engine is there, but it is inanimate" (2004, 40).

Let us now enter the institutions of the European Union, where we have the laboratory of Europe. Here, different nationalities overlap, and the individuals whose common point is European membership live and work together (see also Zabusky 2000). Thus these institutions, and particularly the Commission of Brussels, offer the best observatory for those who wonder about common cultural identity in the EU, since here we are in the presence of a European corps of civil servants who have a different status than national civil servants. I was struck by this ironic and disillusioned remark of one of my interlocutors at the Commission: "We are angels with no body in a world without territory." It deserves some comment because it clearly shows the difficulty that the "makers of Europe" have in finding their place, while they never stop being challenged and criticized by the representatives of national interests.

Europe is distinguished from traditional community groupings by two specific features: from the point of view of space, it is a large-scale community, including a multiplicity of populations and different traditions; from the point of view of time, we are dealing with a community in construction, which is defined as perpetually in process, tending toward an ideal whose realization is constantly deferred. These original characteristics have considerable implications regarding the representations of membership or common identity that individuals can construct.

Europe signifies a change of scale, which as a consequence leads to the deterritorialization of Community practices. The best expression of such deterritorialization is the nomadism of the members of the European Parliament, who are always on the move between Strasbourg and Brussels, when they are not at a meeting somewhere else in Europe. The lack of a center and blurred boundaries make the position of landmarks or "signs of identity" problematic for all those who desperately seek some anchorage. In the case of civil servants, living together in Brussels means sharing the common negative point of residing abroad (with the exception of the Belgians, of course) and being a foreigner in a city where Eurocrats are often criticized. The problems of multiple languages further contribute to a feeling of lost points of reference experienced by European officials.

The example of the European Parliament is enlightening (see Abélès 1992). It is a real tower of Babel, where shifting from one language to another neutralizes debate. The plenary meetings often take the form of a succession of monologues. From time to time, when two deputies of the same country speak one after the other, one foresees the beginning of more spontaneous discussion. The community of language allows direct exchanges and supports a certain freedom of tone: the speakers call upon the same vocabulary, with the same type of references. They operate in an identical universe of speech. Because each country's political language mobilizes a differ- ent rhetoric, certain subtleties are almost impossible to translate across linguistic and political cultural divides. There is no longer any exchange, but isolated speeches placed next to each other at the expense of global meaning and collective stakes. It even resembles at times—because of the various questions dealt with—a surrealist construction, a catalogue à la Prévert. Pluralism effectively becomes an important factor contributing to opacity. Therefore, community identity should not be conceived as a kind of Hegelian going beyond of existing cultural realities. More modestly, what is managed inside the European institutions is a universe of compromise where the conjugation of identities is carried out in a primarily pragmatic mode.

Are there nevertheless collective symbols which can be used as reference, or even orientation, for those engaged in Community practice today? In the first instance, the answer would be negative. The imagery of the instituted Europe is desperately poor. In contrast to the French Republic, which found in Marianne a substantial incarnation (see Agulhon 1989), the European Community seems to be satisfied only with the flag and the anthem.

Are there no other identity markers and references? It seems that one does exist, the "European idea," which the practitioners of Europe refer to as a powerful guide for their actions. In fact, in the day-to-day work of the Commission, the material constraints, the discipline, the weight of every-day routine seem to be articulated by a nonmaterial invest-ment which takes its origin in this "idea of Europe." This 66 idea is as regulatory as it is disincarnated. No one waits for Europe to exist; one builds it up every day. Under these con-ditions, it appears that Europe functions in large part as an "ideal," a concept under which Maurice Godelier (1984) sub-sumes the products of thought in its activities of representa-tion, interpretation, organization, and legitimation.

As a project, Europe combines humanist and rationalist connotations. It corresponds to the affirmation of the ideas of Enlightenment and Reason. It means the emancipation of particularisms in the name of a triumphant universalism. It is also about the primacy of Human Rights. The idea of Europe wants to be synonymous or coterminous with mod-ernism. The priority given to economics is constantly oper-ating in the discourses which celebrate the ideal of a com-munity. For most of the civil servants I met, Europe is less a territory than a method. More than a system of value, prop-erly speaking, it corresponds to a philosophy of action based on the realization of a project which directs the individual's ideals. In such a philosophy the symbolic dimension has no place. The emblem and the few rituals that exist are simple operational artifacts which express, more or less effectively, a rational will.[1] What has been called a "symbolic deficit" in fact seems to correspond to the absence of a coherent set of political concepts and discourses. Everything is working as if Europe were destined to remain a virtual object.

Another identity landmark is contained in the reference to the *Community Interest*. This notion, which is omnipresent in Commission discourse, sustains the process of differentiation between the EU and the other economic powers, most notably the United States and Japan. The notion of a common good is also used in the dialogue between the Community and the member states. I observed how the notion of "Community interest" was advocated during the negotiation with the member states to define the level of European subsidies given to each country under regional policy. In this particular context, it was necessary to satisfy the different needs of the member states. In order to implement a fair distribution, however, it was also necessary to take into account the notion of a superior interest. To take a decision from the point of view of the Community interest meant also following up a policy orientation in order to reduce regional disparities and achieve the necessary transfers for regions to adapt to the Single Market. It meant the simultaneous identification and prioritization of real needs in the countries, at both the regional and national levels. From their side, the member states

1. See Shore and Black (1994) for an exploration of the efforts made in Brussels to instill a European cultural identity among citizens.

put forward the principle of subsidiarity, which, as a consequence, introduced more flexibility for the Community to deal with regional and national problems. During the preparation and the conduct of the negotiation, the opposition between the Community interest and subsidiarity was observed in operation.

To a certain extent, the Community is, to quote Claude Lévi-Strauss (1950), a "floating signifier." He uses this concept to designate notions which are both essential and vague, allowing for their evocation alone to be of great significance. It is similar to the case of the *mana*, which somehow stitches together indigenous discourses (Lévi-Strauss 1950, xlix). In this sense *mana* has an excess of meaning which gives value to the word used in a political context, as well as in its invocation in magic and rituals. From *mana* to Community interest, the distance is huge, but the essential point is the marking function and the power of acknowledgment which are attributed to this concept. The usefulness of this concept may be seen in the debate about the Structural Funds, which highlights the growing importance of subsidiarity against the background of the danger of the renationalization of Community policies. On the other hand, one of the implications of the recourse to this concept is to affirm the reality of a properly European interest.

The consciousness of a common belonging therefore finds in the invocation of a Community interest, and in reference to the European idea, the possibility of affirming itself against what is established as otherness (that of nation-states as opposed to Community) and as particularisms (the national histories as opposed to modernity). We cannot assert here and now that what is happening is the production of a European identity. On the contrary, the practice of the European institutions dramatically demonstrates the effects of deterritorialization which are created in part by Europe-building. From an anthropological viewpoint, one may consider deterritorialization as an enriching and stimulating factor (see also Appadurai 1996).

Cultural pluralism does not produce only centrifugal effects. Learning relativism, as can be observed in Community institutions, is one of the most interesting aspects of the process of pluralization. It implies a continuous questioning about methods, ways of thinking, and management which in a national context are supposed to be "natural" and legitimate, all but preventing any form of questioning. The situation in Community institutions induces the need to compromise between different ways of facing problems, on different grounds (such as economic, environmental, audiovisual, etc.). At the Community level, dossiers acquire a higher complexity because they must account for different national regulatory arrangements. The material interests of the social categories affected (such as fishermen, farmers, miners, or bankers) also vary from one country to another. At the same time, national analysis and perspectives may diverge because of the weight of cultural traditions (for instance the northern and southern member states of Europe do not share the same viewpoint regarding ecology) and the political dividing lines do not necessarily coincide from one state to another (see for instance the case of the media).

Members of Parliament (MEPs) learn in practice the meaning of cultural complexity, and they are sometimes confronted with a very difficult choice between what is best for Europe and what is dictated by their national affiliation. In political debates, the fact that European parliamentary groups exist does not necessarily produce common positions. These positions can be the outcome of very laborious compromises, which may reflect the differences between national political traditions and the apparent similarity of parliamentary party orientation. It is quite striking that political practices at the European level imply the primacy of compromise and negotiation. In parliamentary committees or in the plenary sessions, there is less of an air of confrontation and more a sense of perpetual negotiation between rival powers. Similarly, within each political group what is primarily sought is compromise between national delegations.

Thus, bargaining is an essential component of European political and administrative activity. As Robert Keohane and Stanley Hoffmann (1991, 17) have pointed out, interstate bargains are the necessary conditions for European integration. When one underlines the role of lobbies in Brussels and in the corridors of the Parliament, one refers to the exponential growth of the firms and consultants working for the interest groups of the different member states. But one may simultaneously indicate that lobbyism, as a typical operation of influence, as a pragmatic way of solving problems, and as the embodiment of the primacy of informal relationships, has progressively become the main feature of European political practice. MEPs must become experts in lobbying, bargaining, and compromising, or else they cannot leave their mark in this arena. Rather than observing real political debate in the Parliament, one can see a small group of specialists in a permanent quest for compromise. The generalized bargaining leads to a progressive loss of political content, thereby obscuring the traditional oppositions which demarcate the political domain.

Community practices look like a large "do-it-yourself," where one tries to fashion new conceptions of language, politics, and administration. The written production (notes, rules, official documents) which comes out of the never- ending mixing of cultures is often considered esoteric, because for many it is simply not comprehensible. However, it is precisely because European writers take into account the difference of languages and the need to compensate for the difficulties of translation that such a jargon has come into being (see Bellier 1995). Eurospeak is the emblem of the multicultural job demanded in European institutions. Some observers notice a movement toward homogenization which would be characterized by a global impoverishment of meaning. "In the Commission, gray is the dominant tone," said one of my interlocutors. If there is any sense to a Community culture, it is that of the lowest common denominator. This is the image of a somewhat sterile world, though it does not exclude the possibility for individual imagination.

But the greatest originality of these political places is that a certain type of practice was gradually invented in them, a practice we can approach in two ways. Initially, by observing and analyzing the *conceptual* production and semantics, which is undoubtedly the quintessence of European capacity. The way in which domains are conceptually framed at the Community level has considerable consequences for both the legislation of the various member countries as well as for the everyday life of their citizens.

A good example is the case of the Public Services, which have been the object of Brussels' preoccupations and the work of the Commission these last years. The sectors of energy, transportation, communications, and municipal services are all distributed through networks. More than other services they concern the collectivity as a whole. But the regulation and management of their infrastructure, services, and networks vary widely from one European country to another. In the French case, the concept of *service public* is highly codified. It implies simultaneously the consideration of the general interest and the reference to a public authority (see Thiry 1994). The British use the notion of "public utility" to qualify the activities which provide those services that are considered essential. As with French public services, British public utilities play an essential role in economic development. The need for regulation and public controls is also well acknowledged. The deregulation and privatization program which has been implemented in the United Kingdom, in the sectors ruled until then by public monopolies such as British Telecom and British Gas, accentuated the contrasts between the French orientation and what is usually characterized as the "Anglo-Saxon" one, in reference to the American and British models. In the domain of public services, France and the United Kingdom are situated on the opposite ends of a large spectrum. In Germany, the local authorities are given a real power of definition and control of the public services and the nation-state stays in the background. In southern Europe, however, central authorities are in the foreground. Obviously, diversity reigns across Europe in the area of public services, reflecting the range of cultural and institutional traditions.

These maturely negotiated concepts of framing are to some extent the rock on which any form of regulation is built. As a result, a certain overall vision arises, concretized by the directives in their own ways. Here is what leads to a specific problem: that of the relevance of concepts and values which were negotiated within the Community framework in a national context where they can be shifted. Under these circumstances, observers also should accept the idea of a "bizarre" Europe, which generates strange notions, such as the "êtres de raison," the "chimeras" that Spinoza proposed when he was referring to square circles and other creations of the human understanding. The Community is the melting pot of national cultures which are sometimes very dissimilar.

We can also characterize the practices of these new political spaces as producing not only concepts, but also *causes*, in the sense that we take a position for or against a cause. Or in the sense that one pleads for a good or a bad cause. Cause implies an engagement, and it offers material for public demonstrations. For example, one protests in front of the Parliament by showing an enormous blue whale that symbolizes the harm done to this species in the absence of sufficient compulsion to protect it. But in parallel, there is the advocacy work entrusted to experts, such as members of NGOs and deputies. European political spaces are well suited to the invention of a practice centered on causes (humanitarian, environmental) that have a tremendous capacity to mobilize people.

Go to Brussels today: you will find—in addition to the official institutions—lobby offices, and also all the NGOs that animate the alter-globalization dispute and whose representatives weigh in on the development of European directives. These actors, who can shift from being the manager of an NGO to serving as a eurofonctionnaire, and vice versa, play a focal role in the invention of political know-how which borrows from the modes of action specific to Great Britain and certain countries of northern Europe. They also take part in the development of new practices and transnational networks. European institutions thus have been more than a sounding board of civil society. In reality, they are where we identified the causes that moved to the center of public debate. Sometimes they lead to a rise in power of new actors even on the national political landscape—such as the Green party in France.

One of the most interesting aspects of Europe in construction relates to its mode of historicity. Everything occurs as if the Community were condemned to live perpetually in a headlong rush toward an unknown. Europe is the secular arm of a project whose completion is always being deferred. A movement of dehistoricization corresponds to the process of deterritorialization. In the communities traditionally studied by Europeanist anthropologists, on the contrary, tradition plays a fundamental part. It operates as a unifying theme which directs individual destinies. These societies have a "long memory" (Zonabend 1979): a memory that is the omnipresent counterpoint to daily activity. This is shown by the importance of genealogies and prestige granted to the ancestral, as well as symbolic elaborations and myths celebrating the high doings of the pioneers. When upheavals intervene within the community, it is once again by turning to the past that one gives oneself the means to understand the risks of the present. Tradition indicates current events; it gives them meaning and makes it possible to control—to a certain extent—their contingency. Far from being fixed in place, tradition is the object of a permanent invention, as the continual modification of symbols and rituals eloquently testifies.

This dialectic of the present, memory, and tradition constitutes a fascinating anthropological object in itself. The fact that it is not found in the representations of the experts of Europe deserves to be emphasized. One never stops evoking European "construction," and this term alone merits analysis. The Community is experienced like a building site by its craftsmen. It is not even imagined that this construction will one day be finished. Even better: it is the prospect of the future which gives meaning to this process. Only then will the European Union have arrived at its goal, and integration will finally be realized. But this horizon remains remote and unspecified. Unlike existing states, the EU is experienced as a dynamic process tending toward a goal it is still far from achieving. This incompletion is an essential datum for those who want to understand the operating method of European institutions. It implies the absence of any stable frame of reference and an ever-present prospect of the rise in power of a construction for which no one knows the final configuration. *The representation of time in the European Community is thus completely different from that which prevails in traditional communities. It is entirely directed toward the future.* This is what makes it possible for the craftsmen of Europe to resist the movements of backward flow and resistance to the EU that one periodically observes. The last fifty years are presented as a succession of meaningful accelerations, with the Schuman plan, the treaties of Rome, the integration of new member states, the signature of the Single European Act and the Maastricht treaty. Between each one of these advances, periods of frustration occur. The machine seems to have jammed, and we sink into euro-pessimism or even euro-skepticism.

In the services of the Commission within the Parliament, this type of alternation is sometimes difficult to bear, and the invocation of the future offers the most effective means to deal with this situation. Europe is experienced as a project whose due date is constantly deferred. Civil servants' and elected Community officials' actions are guided by this assumption of the future. Everyone insists on the fact that the situation is not frozen: even the institutions in which they work could still experience significant changes. Unlike national parliaments, the European Assembly does not yet have stable and well-defined attributes. The appearance of new procedures (cooperation, joint decision making) enabled it to extend its field of competency, and the horizon remains open. The role of the Commission is still discussed today, and it is likely to evolve. The institutional future of the EU remains open; in the same way, great uncertainty reigns regarding the final borders that the Community will give itself. The open debate on the integration of Turkey is significant in this respect.

Community membership is therefore experienced in the mode of incompletion. The absolute power of the present and the insistent invocation of the future are in the middle of the daily representations of EU experts. At the Commission, one likes to work with a sense of urgency; this organization is particularly powerful when it assigns short-term objectives. The word "finalize" appears often in the vocabulary of civil servants. Whether it concerns a file, a meeting, or a negotiation in progress, it is important to finish within the deadlines; it is necessary that the action undertaken is carried out. The various European authorities work permanently under the pressure of the calendar. Moreover, the Commission gave itself a calendar when it proposed the Single European Act. The most spectacular aspect of this initiative was to establish a deadline for realizing the Single European Market.

This is how the European Union is built—pushing forward without ever turning around. "We're driving without a rearview mirror," explains a senior official. The absence of a strong referent—which the State with its rules and government represents for national civil servants—becomes palpable. The Commission seems unable to look back on itself, and a large number of its officials have difficulty locating themselves historically. It is as if Europe has to reinvent itself each day and affirm its eternal youth. We seem to ignore the work of memory, so that each successive crisis is neutralized by the cover of memory lapse. The reference to the past is limited to a short evocation of the founding fathers; no sign testifies to the presence of tradition. Any reference to the latter seems incongruous in such a context. This deficit of tradition and the absence of reflexivity in regard to the past characterize the relationship of the European institutional operation to time. We also insist on the importance of the dialectic between present and future which models the future of political Europe. A rigorous analysis could not underestimate the importance taken by the virtual dimension. The political process takes place under the sign of a double indetermination in regard to its definitive form (a new species of nation-state, a federation of states, a postnational structure?) and in regard to the number of participants (where will the enlargement stop?).

We are thus dealing with a mechanism that produces massive political effects, but which remains, strictly speaking, unnamable and indefinite. The introduction of the fuzzy concept of governance testifies to the difficulty of simultaneously apprehending the place of European power and the unity of a project which would direct it. We are in the realm of the emergent and the virtual of what may one day be a unified global political reality. The permanent presence of an open field of problems which now includes an entire discourse on "the absence of response to problems" is revealing. The virtual dimension and the relation to time that it constitutes draws us definitively away from the vision of progress that once prevailed. It obliges us to reflect on what we will define, for want of anything better, as the contemporary "temporalization" of politics, in reference to the concept introduced by the philosopher Reinhart Koselleck. The ideal system produced in the Community universe puts us directly in the virtual realm. The absolute power of the planner and the calendar causes events that have not yet occurred to seem like a present reality, as we saw in the case of the single currency, the EU's expansion, and more recently in the constitutional treaty.

The situation is not without analogy in the field of sciences where, to cite a recent example, cloning is now part of current events, well before the experiment has been tried on humans. What counts is that the presence of the future models and contextualizes the experience of the present. *We understand better why the question of Europe's final political shape is always deferred. It is that the power of the system lies in the mixture which it carries out between the virtual and the real.* The virtual realm limits violent reactions much more effectively than the production of a political order which would solidify relations and could cause arduously controllable reactions of rejection: we are familiar with the hesitancy of the majority of member states to give up all or part of their sovereignty. Unidentified, the European political object finds its effectiveness optimal. It determines national evolutions. It inflects the deal without being affected by the reactions it generates. It is not a paradox to note that the omnipresence and the performance of political Europe have depended in part on virtual dimensions and the uncertainty that characterize it. From this point of view, the anthropology of the present and the contemporary cannot escape a reflection on temporalization. The intertwining of the future and the present, the virtual and the real, has therefore become a component of the Community political process.

This is what makes it possible for Europe to continue advancing until it obtains a constitution which further concretizes the integration of European states. At the same time, this progression of the EU does not provoke the enthusiasm of European citizens. In 2003, according to Eurobaromètre, only 41 percent of them said they had confidence in the European Union. Less than one citizen out of two felt that membership in the EU was a good thing. The national referendums organized to ratify the constitutional treaty were distinguished by impressive rates of abstention. That means that European governance is still a remote reality in the public's opinion. Citizens have some difficulty truly adapting to Europe. Although many public spaces for debate exist, they are mostly occupied by elites (parliamentarians, lobbyists, civil servants). Common man remains removed from these spaces, and periodically one sees the puffs of resentment in regard to the Eurocrats "locked up in their ivory tower." What does this situation show? In itself, the gap between citizens and Europe's leading authorities corresponds to the cleavage between governed and governing specific to modern nations. Politics has entered the era of suspicion: it never appears capable of sufficiently responding to the request of transparency produced by the hypermediatization of public life.

In the contemporary shape of representative government that Bernard Manin defines as a "democracy of the public"

(1997), the link between governed and governing takes place through interactive television—the communication experts take an increasingly eminent place as leaders are required to be "media figures." Power becomes more and more personalized, and yet the distance between a political-media elite and the rest of society continues to grow. In the democracy of parties, leaders were above all militants, which tended to bring them closer to voters. The "breakdown of representation" diagnosed by Pierre Rosanvallon (1998, 334) lies in the growing gap between power and citizens. One of the outstanding features of this "democracy of the public" is that the deliberative process develops outside traditional institutions. Political leaders consult lobbies and associations directly, and their discussion is brought to the public through television. Whence the perpetually deceptive side of this new political arrangement: it seems as if the reporting of events in real time and the visual omnipresence of decision makers were going to offer us a real intimacy with the public realm; and ultimately this does not happen.

Under these conditions, one part of Europeans' dissatisfaction in regard to the EU's form of government is related to the crisis of political representation that the majority of the Western countries have experienced. This same crisis is simply reproduced on a larger scale in the EU. There remains, however, another kind of frustration which lies in the more or less confused perception that a function of power exists, but that it does not correspond to the governmental paradigm of the nation-state. Everyone feels that politics has migrated toward other places, as shown by the frequent reference to

"Brussels," which symbolizes the existence of a different configuration, both omnipresent and imperceptible. We could represent displacement into institutional terms: the European Union would thus be identifiable with a form of federalism. Certain authors define it as "intergovernmental federalism" (Croisat and Quermonne 1996, 148); others note that "the convergence of public politics . . . and their overlapping led, in the absence of arbitration from the top, to a cooperative federalism without a state" (Mény et al. 1995, 345). These definitions are partially unsatisfactory because they do not deal with the specificity of the displacement which has occurred. If the public has the feeling that real power is in the hands of a technocracy only partially controlled by European governments, this reflects the difficulty the latter has to significantly influence the choices that are made by the initiatives of the Commission. That's only natural, one would say, since it is the Commission that has power to make proposals for directives which are then presented at the European Council, where the representatives of member states sit.

But there are cases where the impact of this transnational institution—the Commission—is thrown into the open. This was the case in 2005 for the project of the Bolkestein directive on services. It stipulated that European service providers would only be subjected to the law of their country rather than to that of the member states where they offered their services. This measurement, part of a neoliberal position, was at the origin of a general outcry among all those who protested against the risks of social dumping. The European Trade Union Confederation denounced these policies of reform that have "become a code for endless deregulation and flexibility, the reduction of wages and the weakening of workers' rights, as well as the dismantling of social security." For his part, José Barroso, the president of the Commission, declared, "We must have a single market of services; it will have to be primarily based on the principle of the country of origin with suitable guarantees" (March 14, 2005). This famous principle was at the heart of the controversy over the text. Even if the project envisaged permanent exemptions from the principle of the country of origin concerning certain public services, such as the postal service or gas and electricity distribution, it diverged from the prevailing design in a country like France, where services cannot be sold off to companies who are able to propose more advantageous conditions for consumers because they pay low wages and offer their employees reduced social protection.

The controversy around the Bolkestein directive developed in France well after it was adopted by the Prodi Commission, with the endorsement of the two French commissioners. At the time that the Dutch commissioner Frits Bolkestein proposed the directive to the interior market, he had by no means caused an uproar. His colleagues adopted it without much opposition. We can assume that the French government (which was divided at the time, with a center-right president and a Socialist prime minister) had been informed of the proposal. None of the national leaders, however, thought it best to express their disapproval. It was as if we had brutally discovered—in the tempest of the referendum campaign—the existence of a text that had been the subject of a lengthy process of development before being submitted to the authorities of the European Union. However, even legally speaking, there was a good deal at stake. This point was highlighted by the report of the French State Council, which was consulted concerning the Bolkestein directive, and which stressed the legal risks arising from a generalized application of the principle of the service provider's country of origin. The directive created a situation in which it would be possible for a craftsman to sell his services abroad while only having to respect the legislation of his own country. "If the principle of territorial application of criminal law were called into question, owing to the fact that national law would be paralyzed with regard to a service provider acting in France, it would be appropriate to take the difficulties which would result from it into full account," indicated the State Council's report. Doesn't this report indicate the way in which the implementation of a Community directive can collide with national jurisdiction and thus weaken the state mechanism?

Even though the directive was finally rejected by the European Council, the concern over services that it caused is symptomatic. *This disquiet is related to the sometimes painful realization of an irreversible change in scale in the approach to certain questions of public interest.* With traditional powers being pushed around, arbitrations are occurring in places other than those to which people normally pay attention: everyone can now note the concrete effects of the displacement of politics. Displacement is the vector of uncertainty. Paradoxically, the more Europe succeeds, the more it disquiets. After two major advances—enlargement of the EU and the single currency, which, at the time when they happened, did not pose a problem—it was precisely *then* that one saw a violent reaction of rejection in France and the Netherlands. It is as if Europe, by projecting us almost mechanically toward an elsewhere whose direction is out of our control, caused an intense negative reactivity. The European case, however, simply illustrates a more general tendency—one that it is essential to fully comprehend.

4 Understanding the Displacement of Politics: From Convivance to Survival

Alongside the European project, the end of the twentieth century saw a growth in the strength of a set of transnational organizations with no explicit governmental aims, such as the World Bank, the International Monetary Fund (IMF), and the World Trade Organization (WTO). In the context of a fluid society, it appears that these organizations, whose players remain anonymous for the general public, have taken a preeminent place. Today they seem omnipresent and impenetrable, enjoying visibility as a result of their effects on the world. They escape the usual issue of democratic representation, and it is revealing that they are seen as condensing power and authority to such a high degree.

In just a few years, these organizations have become a target for all those who denounce the social and cultural ravages of the new neoliberal paradigm. It is no accident that the meetings of the WTO have sparked off major demonstrations. The 1999 Seattle demonstrations unquestionably marked a turning point, with the rise in power of a vast alterglobalization movement. When we look back over the last ten years, we are struck by the remarkable conjunction of two phenomena. On the one hand, a certain number of the key elements of governance, in areas as diverse as the economy, the environment, and human rights, have been partly taken over by these transnational organizations. On the other hand, a battlefront has developed that designates these new powers as the main target.

There is a dual displacement, then, in both governmentality and resistance. Of course, national powers still maintain a strong influence on the functioning of these organizations. It is not by chance that Paul Wolfowitz was named the head of the World Bank in 2005; like Robert McNamara before him, he incarnates the weight of the United States on the international scene. But doesn't the designation of such a high ranking American policy maker to lead the World Bank illustrate the key place that this institution occupies within the global economy? The present moment can be characterized by the emergence of a new political stage whose true place can be gauged by examining confrontations, such as the conflicts that occurred during the WTO meetings and the G7 summits. Davos and Porto Alegre have become the symbols of this political displacement and of the way in which traditional intranational antagonisms have not just acquired a new dimension but also, for better or worse, reflect a new political vision of the world. This vision is utterly different from the one that prevailed for so long within parties and other organizations that were, until now, at the heart of the power balance in their respective countries.

In other words, when we talk about political displacement, an analysis in terms of institutions and players can only imperfectly account for what has been rumbling below the surface for some fifteen years. We can measure the limits of this approach through the debate it gives rise to, which concerns above all the issue of knowing whether state sovereignty is threatened by globalization. Here, we reason exclusively in reference to power balances, at the risk of losing sight of what is really at stake in the dynamic that can no longer be ignored, in which both citizens and their leaders are involved. Must we restrict ourselves to a way of thinking that focuses entirely on the power of states versus the power of international and supranational structures?

Legitimate though it is, the interest in this question risks masking a deeper phenomenon. The reorganization of the "powers that be" and the increasing power of the transnational on a global scale are only the tip of the iceberg. Deep down, we are dealing with the very meaning we give today to the business of politics and our perception of the political dimension. Politics is in a process of radical transformation. Its displacement is not limited to the appearance of a new political scene in which the old institutional powers are replaced by newer ones, more able to handle the change in scale brought on by globalization; it is not as though we had simply moved out the old dressers to make way for an enormous clean-up, as if the content of the drawers remained the same.

We are dealing with something completely different—the new part of this displacement is the *content* of the drawers. And it is precisely because these new elements did not fit in the old dressers that they had to be replaced. I use this metaphor to illustrate the following: this political displacement is determined by a global redefinition of the meaning and aims of political action. This redefinition is not simply cognitive. It also shows up in ways of acting and in organizational and institutional constructions, in the positioning of issues that will be a focus for public debate, and in the construction of the type of place where this debate will happen. This theory is heavy with consequences: *it effectively implies that the emergence of a new, transnational stage is the consequence rather than the cause of a profound transformation of our relationship to politics.* This means that, in research, the institutional process must give way to an investigation of our perception of politics. It is here that the displacement, whose most visible effects we have already spotted, is really happening.

In these conditions, it is best to take a step back regarding ideas as omnipresent as those of state and sovereignty. The experience of anthropologists has shown that the state's absorption of political activity—the fact that the state became the place of politics—is the result of a historical process and thus corresponds to an ephemeral era. They have clearly shown that the state is only one form of government among many others. Hastily associating modernity and the preeminence of the state has the danger of making it impossible to understand a change that actually leads to a displacement of the state as the "political place."

As Michel Foucault recommended, "The analysis in terms of power must not postulate as given the sovereignty of the State, the form of law or the total unit of domination;

these are none other than the terminal forms" (1976, 120). If political anthropology has contributed to de-reifying the political dimension, by showing the degree to which a focus on the form of state control had ultimately obscured the real diversity of the figures of power, Foucault, for his part, has underlined the need to ask the question of "how" and look at the exercise of power. Reflecting on power as an action—as a "way of acting upon actions" (2000b, 341)—was also to challenge the traditional instruments of the political theories that "had recourse only to ways of thinking about power based on legal models, that is: What legitimizes power? Or they had recourse to institutional models, that is: what is the state?"(2000b, 327). This meant that we had to remove the legal and institutional biases from our approach to politics.

A focal issue in this new perspective is that of governing. Here we come to a theme dear to Foucault: the art of governing, or in other words the practices by which we manage to "structure the possible field of action of others" (2000b, 341). One of the difficulties encountered by any anthropology of power comes from the permanent overlap that exists between "the art of governing" together—of concrete procedures that define the field of power balances—and a theory of sovereignty that claims both to establish the legitimacy of these procedures and to extend their meaning, even if it means postulating a transcending horizon—a "hereafter" of power. The phenomenon of divine kingship in African societies offers a good example of how power is embedded in a metaphysics of sovereignty.

As far as politics in "near" societies is concerned, the entanglement of power and the discourse of sovereignty is so strong that only an effort of "defamiliarization" allows one to highlight its displacement. Foucault made history play the role of the operator, allowing him to take a distant view of contemporary power and bring its constituent elements to light. In the seventeenth and eighteenth centuries, a new mechanism of power was invented that applied to people rather than to land. On the contrary, the traditional theory of sovereignty is linked to a power exercised foremost on the land and its products, and not on the bodies of subjugated individuals. In this vision, power aims to seize goods and wealth—not working hours: "This theory makes it possible for power to be based on and around the physical existence of the sovereign and not at all on and around continuous and permanent surveillance systems" (2001, 186).

Foucault shows how what he calls a "power mechanism" applying to bodies rather than to land was put in place in the same period. The aim of this power was to "obtain work and time from bodies rather than goods and wealth" (2001, 186). It was to be the key instrument of the development of industrial capitalism. This disciplinary power does not emerge from the traditional theory of sovereignty. The "disciplines" standpoint is not that of the law; it refers to nature and aims to standardize behavior. Medicine, medicalization, and "human sciences" all contribute to this structure.

Beyond bringing to light the emergence of disciplinary techniques centered on the individual and his body, Foucault also shows how a new technology, dealing with men in their multiplicity—the population—was put in place at the end of the eighteenth century. This technology, which he calls biopolitics, deals with the population as both a scientific and a political issue. The interest taken in demography, the development of public hygiene, the institutions of assistance and insurance and the taking into account of the relationship between man and the environment define a new configuration where the disciplinary dimension fades in favor of a project that aims to prolong life and regulate biological mechanisms. With the rise in the power of capitalism, these disciplinary work technologies acquired less direct procedures that allowed power to be taken over men as a group of living beings. Man was no longer just subjugated in his individual singularity, he was also controlled as a specimen of a population of living beings: the population as an undivided entity was the new subject of biopolitical sovereignty.

While disciplinary techniques were especially associated with humans seen in their corporal individuality — the human as a body — biopolitical techniques integrate the multiplicity of men into a global whole by focusing on man as a species. Unlike the disciplinary approach, which stuck to "anatomo-politics," biopolitics implies authority taking control of the processes affecting life, from birth to death (sickness, old age, handicaps, environmental factors, etc.) — which, although absolutely random at an individual level, have, as a collective phenomenon, decisive economic and political effects. The birth of police science and the premises of the politics of public health have progressively placed biological or natural life among the technical management preoccupations, calculations, and forecasts of the state. The conformity of lifestyle and customs of its political subjects preoccupies the state far less than their birth, their registration in the political registers of nationality, and the demography of their biological life.

At a biopolitical level, the individual is no longer targeted, but is considered by the biopolitical norm as a specimen of a population whose movements, both internal and external, must be regulated — diminution, growth, geographical movement. In contrast to traditional sovereignty, characterized by the power to make die or let live, power is now defined by its capacity to make live or let die. Far from being in contradiction with this redefinition of power oriented toward life, state racism, having been responsible for millions of deaths, has proved itself actively involved in the issue of the "biological strengthening" (Foucault 1997, 230) of a population.

We could read Foucault's work on biopower as a sort of genealogy of the modern welfare state, whose particular rationality he tries to bring out. But throughout the investigation, the trail he follows is that of the way in which the "the tricky adjustment between political power wielded over legal subjects and pastoral power wielded over live individuals" has been implemented (2000a, 307). He describes two separate traditions — and, beyond that, two sets of perceptions — that never align with each other. On the one hand is a perception of power or the relationship of the government to the governed, illustrated through the metaphor of the shepherd leading his flock. The pastoral theme is prevalent in ancient oriental societies. The other tradition, illustrated notably by Plato in *The Statesman*, sees in the art of governing the capacity to achieve the unity of the city—to "weave the finest of fabrics" (cited in Foucault 2000a, 307). The welfare state could be said to constitute an unusual moment in history, in that it managed to bring the two perceptions together in a single, cohesive whole—the state as "centralized and centralizing power," orientated toward the citizen, and "pastorship" as the "individualizing power" (2000a, 300), aimed at individuals.

We might ask ourselves whether this harmony between pastoral power and the centralizing state has disappeared today. *It is as though a dislocation were taking place in our perception and experience of the political dimension between what comes under the rubric of citizen/individual and what relates to the biopolitical subject.* Let us not be mistaken about my use of Foucauldian categories. I am aware that these ideas were developed to account for the complex relationship between the state and the individual—by avoiding the reduction of power merely to its repressive dimension, as ideological discussions of totalitarianism sometimes do. Foucault never tires of repeating that highlighting the negative aspect of power and interpreting it unequivocally in terms of law and proscription leads up a blind alley, by portraying a face-off with no solution, between an all-powerful sovereign and a subject forced into voluntary servitude. The philosopher's entire efforts have centered on bringing out the importance of this relationship as a producer of modes of subjectification that condition the existence and lifestyle of individuals. At the same time—and this may be one of the limitations of the Foucauldian approach—the issue of subjects' relationship with politics is only tackled from the point of view of the relationship between the state and individuals, under the concepts of power and resistance.

It is as though, in the final instance, it is the sovereign power that pulls the strings. The projector is permanently trained on the polymorphous disciplines of power and the mechanisms they put into play. Foucault barely touches upon the elements that he designates as forms of political subjectification. Jacques Rancière (2000) argues that the question of politics understood as "that in which the status of the subject who is apt to act within a community is concerned . . . has never interested Foucault." Foucault's object is not politics, but police, understood as a form of "dividing sensitivities structuring perceptive space in terms of place, functions, aptitudes, etc., with the exclusion of any supplement" (Rancière 2000). The criticism arrives at a sensitive point, by highlighting that Foucault's research concerns above all the control mechanisms over bodies and populations, while ignoring political agency and the subjects involved in it.

The prevalence of the state viewpoint in Foucault's approach should not, however, make us lose sight of how Foucault reintroduces ambivalence into political theory by separating the issues of power and sovereignty. Taking seriously the biopolitical dimension radically complicates the traditional vision of the res publica as a harmonious space where subjects engage in political dialogue, having laid aside all attributes other than those of citizenship. While the author of *Discipline and Punish* does not explain this ambivalence, it is a constant nagging presence in his work. And by taking this ambivalence seriously we can better understand what is being played out today in the "political displacement" that we are facing. We have to look at the current disjunction between the biopolitical point of view and the citizen/individual point of view in its own dynamic. In fact, we can actually speak of a real switch-over, with the rise in power of political representation that puts the preoccupations of life and survival at the heart of political action, while the issue of the city and the relationship of the individual to sovereignty are relegated to the background. The displacement of issues can find another expression in a simple question that we all ask: "What will our world consist of tomorrow?" It is this fundamental anxiety that not only alters our relationship to politics but also determines the space that can be allocated to political activity and the new places in which it is best exercised.

This is demonstrated by a certain number of phenomena that merit analysis from this perspective and that lead us to reflect on what makes up the everyday political reality of each one of us. The French philosopher Bergson spoke of the "immediate data of consciousness." We might paraphrase his expression by considering the "immediate data of politics" — in other words, those preoccupations that are now inseparable from our way of being in society. They all have in common the fact that they cast us beyond the well-defined world of a national community whose history and relative homogeneity within its own borders guarantee permanence and tranquility. It is as though something has become unbalanced, that everyone in his or her own way is trying to comprehend by attributing this situation either to an event (September

11) or to a type of causality that we cannot control (climate change). It is as though the citizen's capacity for initiative were going through an explicit reassertion of powerlessness, tied to the awareness of a radical reappraisal of our terms of belonging. *The other side of this position is a projection toward a vaguer collective interest relating more to survival than to the art of "harmonious living together"* (convivance).

The world of convivance corresponds to a political tradition maintained in the national state framework and centered, above all, on synchronic harmony between beings who operate in the reassuring world of the city, or at least orient their actions according to this perspective, even when they are tearing each other apart in endless conflicts. Convivance does not imply the idea of a world at peace. In fact, it has given rise to sharply contrasting political theories, some emphasizing the role of violence and domination as the regulator of living together, while others base political unity on the determination of a common enemy. There certainly exists a more peaceful vision of convivance, such as that developed by Habermas in his theory of communicative action, which gives a leading role to argumentative procedures—essential instruments, according to this philosopher, in the resolution of conflicts. But we can equally share the point of view of Hobbes, for whom political society derives directly from the destructive impulse inherent in every human being, which leads him into a dog-eat-dog relationship with his fellows. What interests us here is that political theorists have in mind a state of the world that presupposes the actual or potential existence of stable communities. They suggest that the individual's main aim is to preserve this type of community — of which the nation-state represents the most evolved integrative form. In other words, this is saying we are dealing with a type of political action whose "sufficient reason," as Leibniz would have said, is achieving the stable collective.

Let us now imagine a different, even very different, state of affairs, where convivance no longer represents the principal aim of societal beings, and that they have, in fact, established another priority. Let's suppose, for example, that the theories we habitually refer to do not take into account the possibility of such a change of objective. We are disturbed, thrown off balance, and saddened in the face of a state of affairs no one seems to have seen coming. But perhaps, we might object, this situation only appears to be new and we only need to refine the models we already have to grasp its meaning. Such a solution would have the advantage of being less intellectually costly. It would at any rate correspond to the dominant theories of contemporary society. On the contrary, we can see the inadequacy of these theories every time that we tackle the very specific issue of insecurity — which is also localized, since we take the case of France as our starting point. Following this thread, we will find ourselves led to take account of a much more far-reaching set of preoccupations that shape the entire relationship of the individual to politics.

It is interesting to observe that, at the end of the last century, the question of "insecurity" exploded into the French public space as the result of a return of delinquency. Fatalism easily accommodated itself to what seemed like an inescapable outcome of the society of consumption, enrichment, and inequalities. Insecurity was first linked to a question of maintaining the peace. Progressively, however, it became central in political debate, even taking a lead role in the French presidential elections of 2002. In general, insecurity is understood through the lens of harmonious living together (convivance)—hence the fact that we blame the state for its incapacity to maintain harmonious cohabitation between populations living in urban peripheries. We underline the tensions between "autochthones" and "migrants," which feeds the radicalization of discourses demanding more re-pression when confronted with real or imagined threats to civil order.

Curiously, over the last few years, this feeling of insecurity has spread. It was amplified by September 11, 2001, and this event's innumerable repercussions. The omnipresence of the threat was superimposed on the concept of insecurity. Inse-curity has now extended across many fields, covering areas as heterogeneous as nature (the threat of catastrophes), civil order (delinquency and its effects), or employment (transfor-mations of wage-earning and the social protection system). For example, the sociologist Robert Castel explains that when public safety mechanisms tend to be reinforced, one observes instead a true weakening of social protection systems. This corresponds to the erosion of salaried work, which depended on the rights set up by the welfare state. As Castel under-lines, "Through the mutation of capitalism, which began to produce certain effects in the 1970s, we can observe a gener-alized shift of work relations, professional careers, and pro-tections attached to employment. This created a profound dynamic of decollectivization, re-individualization, and inse-curization" (2003, 43).

From insecurity to insecurization: the threat is no longer only about contingency (what can or cannot happen to you). This is what is placed in the middle of individuals' activity, as the product of a transformation of relations of production as inescapable as it is difficult to control. We are, moreover, wit-nessing the emergence of a category of workers who consider themselves to be in a precarious state, because the absence of a well-defined status forces them to live permanently in the uncertainty of the following day. In a working world that is now devoted to flexibility, we can wonder whether precari-ousness is becoming the common condition of the majority of workers. As we see it, the syndrome of insecurity, initially circumscribed within the problems of law and order, became a leitmotiv of modern civilization. We could even wonder whether the multiplication of reasons for anguish ends up structuring political subjectivities around a more general in-terrogation which relates to the future and more precisely to what we could call the conditions of human survival. What prevails today is the problem of survival which directs the way in which we formulate our aspirations and choices within public space.

I must now clarify this concept of survival. Secondly, we will ask ourselves what degree of relevance this notion has from an anthropological point of view — that is, while placing oneself well within this particular case of our developed West-ern societies. It is true that labor casualization, along with the growing sentiment that we are no longer sheltered, corresponds to a precise historical turn. When Habermas writes that "today it is the states that are anchored in the markets rather than the national economies in official borders" (2000, 130), he only takes note of the change in scale that marked the end of the twentieth century, and of the devolution — to global economic actors — of a power that now escapes, in part, traditional political operators.

In the modern configuration, the state — which traditionally had the power over life and death — was given an even heavier responsibility than securing its citizenry's life. This triumph of the welfare state in charge of biopower, will, in the end, not have lasted long, at least on the scale of human history. This is what would explain the rise to power of the theme of survival, which reveals itself through the syndrome of insecurity and in the persistent anguish concerning the durability of our world and our possible future, foretold by growing instability and the recurring threats of large-scale aggression.

The survival issue plainly stands out in even greater relief because of the fact that it corresponds to the weakening of the rock that has represented, for Western societies, the formidable power of a state that is both national and protective. It is hardly surprising that individuals are directly affected by the loss of bearings implicit in such a collapse. In terms of social relationships, there has been a weakening of the collective bond forged in an institutional context whose fragilities are increasingly apparent. In terms of territory, demarcations hitherto relevant to living as a community are melting and opening out onto a world as vast as it is blurred. The state — whatever its successive leaders did with it—had been invested with a network of beliefs and had, in sometimes tense conditions, taken over from religion, which represented considerable symbolic investment (Agulhon 1989). The state represented not only a power of assistance, but also an *insurance* concerning the future. What was disappearing at the end of the twentieth century was "this capacity to control the future" that had characterized the triumph of the welfare state during the years of economic growth following the Second World War, with the hope for social progress as a correlate (Castel 2003). In the new configuration, this very system—which guaranteed the possibility of some consistency between "my present life" and "my future"—is becoming fuzzy. The problem is not one of management of the polis, since the state is still functional in this respect, nor is it a problem of policing. In other words, the subject of harmonious living together (convivance) is not relevant here, and political theory is off balance in the face of a questioning focused primarily on subjects' relationship to the future. The focus on survival bluntly raises this issue, for there is now an element of uncertainty lodged in people's minds, tensely coexisting with the hope— created by technical and scientific advances—that it is possible to live better and longer.

The fact that the future looks like a permanent, pertinent question, in a situation where uncertainty factors are multiplying, is shaping our relationship to politics. I purposely use the idea of "survival" in contrast to the analysis of survival given by Elias Canetti (1984 [1962]). This other type of survival implies a fundamental antagonism between "I" and others. It is associated with power. On the battlefield, the more corpses of my friends and enemies are piled up around me, the stronger I feel; as Canetti explains, "The moment of survival is the moment of power" (227). The quintessence of survival here is invulnerability. Death is behind us and no longer presents a threat because we've defeated it. The issue of survival in the sense I intend reaches into a different temporal realm: we are not in the "afterwards," in the pleasure of the present felt by those who have overcome the gravest peril, expressed, according to Canetti, in a feeling of strength, of sovereignty and "a feeling of being chosen" (228). Here, on the other hand, everything relates back to insecurity, to the uncertainty of a possibly futureless tomorrow. With the damage caused by progress, thanks to insecurity and all its forms, the future is transformed into a threat. How can we banish uncertainty? This is how the vague sense creeps in that no authority can actually deal with the sort of heavy shadow that looms over the present.

Let us return once again to Canetti. By placing the moment of surviving at the center of his reflection, by exalting the pure factuality of a present that temporarily returned obscurity to the specter of death, the author of *Auto-da-Fé* (1984 [1947]) implicitly scoffed at the ideologists of his time, those who sung the praises of human creativity, in the name of the brilliance the future would bring. One of the lessons of Canetti's *Crowds and Power* is that we must certainly not wait for the sun to rise and illuminate the world for centuries to come. "When the concept of the dispossessed proletariat was first advanced and began to take effect, it retained the full optimism of increase. No one supposed for a moment because their lives were miserable, there ought perhaps to be fewer of them," explains Canetti ironically (1984 [1962], 192). He illustrates his skepticism of the programming discourses that hope to transport us out of the contingency of the present, and toward an inevitably utopian universe. The alternative is simple: either we stick to the anthropological evidence, the *hic* and *nunc*, as a self-affirmation, with its correlate of surviving which is always retrospective, or we let ourselves be won over by the ideological mistakes of the professors of the future.

While this vision of the things is not incoherent, it remains unable to deal with the problematic of survival, which implies that concern over the future seized the present, even clouding individual behaviors, and contributed to the rise of new forms of collective mobilization. This overlapping of temporalities occurred along with societal transformations, and without being noticed. But it leads to questionings that we now have some difficulty isolating under distinct rubrics. For example, there was a time—not so long ago—when we could easily designate what preoccupations came from the "private" realm, attributed to certain life choices of the domestic kind, opposed to others that concerned the "public" realm. When anthropologists studied kinship relations, family structures in our societies, no one had the idea to infer—from their investigations and analyses—those elements that could determine collective possibilities relating to the future of the polis. It was only in the so-called "primitive" societies where we agreed to allow for a strong interrelationship between kinship and politics. On the contrary, in our own societies, we never stopped insisting on the autonomy between these different spheres.

What about all this today? We only have to refer to the recent political incidents, in Europe as well as in the United States: one of the debates that provoked the highest mobilization of public opinion in the last several years—even becoming a real electoral issue—concerns marriage between homosexuals. All the politicians, local and national, are taking a position on an issue that had been part of the private realm for a long time. Even better: during the legislative hearings on the proposition of a civil union law (*Pacte civil de solidarité*—PACS) in France, members of the National Assembly confronted each other on the definitions of marriage and family by referring to anthropological and sociological theories, citing the texts of Claude Lévi-Strauss, Françoise Héritier, and Irène Théry. It was not about proving their erudition, but instead trying to outline what would be the domestic group of tomorrow in French society, without which we would risk the progressive disintegration of the frameworks of its reproduction.

It is revealing that the discussion about the PACS provoked not only an animated confrontation within the Assembly, but also protests outside of it. Is it simply a "societal debate," to borrow the language of specialist political commentators? Or should we see in the echo of this kind of debate the hint that politics is being reconfigured through the lens of survival? Certainly, the homosexual marriages celebrated in the United States by the mayor of San Francisco and then in

France by the mayor of Bègles triggered a powerful controversy, provoking reactions of leaders in both countries. During the U.S. presidential election in 2004, the question came up in the debates between George W. Bush and John Kerry.

This example reveals the way in which discourse and political action are assailed by issues that entirely overwhelm their traditional grounds. Is this simply an extension of the subjects treated in the framework of public policies? It is as though these subjects have penetrated all of society's pores, thus generating unseen forms of legislation. The fact that governments and parliaments now take charge of issues regarding mores and customs that used to be addressed by the courts, allowing for a more or less efficient evolution of jurisprudence, must be considered in light of the displacement that profoundly alters our relationship to politics. This hypothesis does not contradict the observation of an extension of the domain of decision. Similarly, this perspective allows us to interpret the increasingly important role granted to expertise in all its forms. This is due not only to the increasing complexity of the objects on which political action is exercised, but also to a major difficulty which relates to the modes of exercise of power and decision. If professional politicians are less comfortable in these fields, it is because of a competency problem. Is it possible to adjudicate, with necessary rigor, on cases that require legal know-how as well as relatively thorough sociological or even philosophical reflection? Hence the need, in order to reinforce legitimacy, to call on experts. But there is more: even in their formulation, the demands coming from society require new forms of decoding and thwart a certain type of discourse to which experienced politicians are accustomed.

The recourse to expertise appears to be the consequence of the complexification of the issues debated in the public sphere. But it corresponds to the growing awareness that some of these issues are undecidable. They are part of the horizon of survival and project us into a time that is not yet ours, but that is likely to become ours, thus causing a violent telescoping of our present. Ulrich Beck describes what he designates the "second modernity" by this omnipresent uncertainty characteristic of "the global risk society." According to him, one of the most spectacular effects of scientific development is to have vastly increased insecurity. In the first modernity, each new advance was presented as the only good solution which could fix the previously outstanding problem. We lived under the standard of progress, without questioning the long-term implications of these discoveries. "In the second modernity, we are in the framework of a radically different game since, no matter what we do, we expect unexpected consequences" (Beck 2003, 207). This obsessive fear of risk culminated in the mad cow affair, when it was shown that the quality of humans' food and consequently their lives were endangered, and all this because of a technology invented by men. It was out of the preoccupation with efficiency that we developed the use of the animal flours to nourish cattle. Epizooty followed from there, and then human contamination.

The repercussions of mad cow were considerable. Today, nobody feels sheltered from the harmful effects of innovations that aim at rationalizing the food industry. The controversies around the importation of transgenic plants in Europe are in this respect significant. Currently, more than a fifth of the world's crops of colza, cotton, and soy are genetically modified, mainly in the United States, Argentina, Canada, and China, and more recently in India, Colombia, and Honduras. The firms which produce genetically modified organisms (GMOS) present them as a formidable innovation because of their capacity to confront natural pests: they resist freezes, overripeness, rot, certain viruses, parasites, weed killers, and desertification. In response to ecologists who denounce the damage of productivism, the developers of GMOS announce a second generation of organisms which will have beneficial effects on the environment. For example, the transgenic pig will be programmed to produce evacuations deprived of phosphates, and we will thus avoid pollution by liquid manure. We are still in the field of probability, and the biotechnological firms praise the quality of GMO, designed to adapt to arid and saline zones, and particularly favorable to the conditions of dryness which prevail in the Third World. However, a more general interrogation of the medium-term effects of the dissemination of transgenic microorganisms has not yet been achieved. This is how the transgenic plants produced by Monsanto grew without insecticide. The plants themselves permanently diffuse a lethal insecticidal toxin for the bee moth, the parasite of corn. We do not yet know if the latter will develop, in time, a resistance to the insecticidal plants.

Biotechnological discoveries, far from calming fears, actually generate new anxieties. GMOS could be representative of the beginning of a solution to Third World difficulties. On the contrary, they can appear as a threat, and a growing part of public opinion denounces the diffusion of these products that it associates with the worst derivatives of modern capitalism, thirsty for profit and indifferent to the future of the planet. This is what characterizes the paradox of modernity: science and technology, far from being welcomed with enthusiasm and gratitude, are now held in suspicion, and sometimes even vigorously challenged. In any case, they contribute more to the sharpening of antagonisms than to the simplification of debates. As Ulrich Beck writes, "Instead of extinguishing political fires, they pour oil on the flames of ethical, ecological, and political controversies" (2003, 208). It is as though catastrophes will be in proportion to the extent of technological innovations, such as with the quasi-panic caused by the anticipation of the year 2000 computer bug. We were already picturing the shattered data-processing programs and the consequences of the bug on whole sectors of the global economy. In other words, the consequence of the generalized computerization of our societies—the result of a series of extraordinary technological exploits—would be the weakening of systems whose operation is now dependent on computing tools. Our reliance on computing provokes a fear of attacks of any kind, which can come just as easily from a young talent (like the inventor of the virus *Iloveyou* which devastated systems in just a few hours) as from organized professionals. We never cease reinforcing the security system. In parallel, in the event of a terrorist attack, companies and banks in capital cities likely to be touched have a replication of their sites and information.

A real spiral of insecurity thus takes shape. Innovation is a vector of risk, despite its defensive core. Everything is done to minimize these risks, but by doing so the feeling of insecurity grows. There is no reason to be surprised if the authorities are increasingly challenged on the way they intend to respond to the entirety of threats—however diffuse they are—weighing on the future. It is in this context that we must interpret the primacy survival takes over harmoniously living together (convivance). It is not so much a question of promoting such or such a model of society more or less apt in ensuring balanced relations *between humans*. What matters now is to *attain harmony between humans and their future*, and confronting *this* challenge seems much more difficult. This results in the distress of political experts, despite their habit of proposing new programs or—more modestly—propositions, at each electoral term. By definition, a programming speech aims at making a situation better than the one that prevails when it is announced. On the survival horizon, however, it is the opposite measure which is essential. It is no longer innovation and improvement which are required. It is not a question of promoting the best, but of avoiding the worst. This is enough to disconcert political leaders who have some difficulty realizing that their efforts to "renew" the approach to problems provokes skepticism, and even derision, among their fellow citizens.

If "modernist" discourse and "social" enunciations no longer have the intended effect, it is not surprising that a previously unseen phenomenon imposed itself in the public sphere, and that this object, by its nature, was supposed to interest scientists and jurists. *The precautionary principle made a noticeable entrance into the official texts of the French Republic.* Unlike other principles which once caused violent antagonisms, as was the case for secularism, we witnessed a true consensus taking shape. To tell the truth, the definition of the precautionary principle simply consists in stipulating that "in the event of serious threats to the environment, it is not necessary to await all the scientific evidence before acting" (Hermitte 2001, 547). But this attitude represents a revolution compared to the traditional approach to technological risks in our societies. Until then, one could put new products on the market without being concerned about their effects. It was only in the event of damage that one sought to determine the causes and to establish a *prevention* policy. We began with a certitude, and it was only if we had succeeded in showing a cause-and-effect relationship that measures were taken. The contaminated blood affair in France illustrates this situation. The first cases of AIDS go back to 1980. Two years later, the hypothesis of a transmissible causal agent by blood was announced. But the discovery of the cause of the disease took place only in 1984, followed by the development of a screening test at the beginning of 1985. Until this time, uncertainty dominated. As can be observed in regard to giving blood, the criteria of donor selection in France and the United Kingdom in 1983 came from the idea of precaution. It was only after 1985 that these measures arose from the idea of prevention. In other words, prevention is inseparable from a context where the risks are known. The concept of precaution implies, on the other hand, a zone of uncertainty. To raise precaution to the dignity of a constitutional principle is not only to recognize the limits of the power of science, but to give politics a new requirement. Politics is faced with situations in which it is enjoined to anticipate and to choose between various possible scenarios, while placing itself on the horizon of the worst.

Along with uncertainty, it is negativity that now constitutes the background of public action: negativity of catastrophes and negativity of techno-scientific innovation regarding its effects on environment and life, without forgetting the lurking evil, concretized in the figure of the terrorist who sows death around him. "Evil exists in the world," writes Jean-Pierre Dupuy, "it has certain effects on the world, but neither the rationalist model nor its critical demystification is able to recognize it" (2002, 31). We can wonder about the recourse to a notion that concerns morals and even theology. We would still not be able to underestimate the impact on public opinion of diagnoses that see a new form of nihilism in terrorism, a nihilism whose reappearance would be only one expression of the obsessing presence of evil in human history. Through these debates, the shared prescience of a permanent threat weighing on humanity and its environment emerges. From a cognitive point of view, several representations telescope into one another, which make us go from the recognition of uncertainty to the realization of a threat and the apprehension of evil. We are negotiating between very different levels: on the one side there is the question of the status of the relationship between science, expertise, and policy, in an increasingly complex universe of decisions. In addition, it is a question of facing the damage of progress, not to mention the black continent of uncertainty, threats of all kinds, and the shade of the evil.

It is not about evaluating the intrinsic rationality of these representations. What interests us is that they feed the problems of survival, that they take part in this search for the least dreadful future. From this point of view, we can consider that the appearance of the precautionary principle, with, as a counterpoint, the implementation of "enlightened catastrophism," according to the eloquent formula of Dupuy, precedes an aggiornamento of political practices. Curiously, this reorientation is configured in ethical terms. Faced with the risks and uncertainties of the future, individuals are called upon to demonstrate a specific quality: responsibility. In the words of Hans Jonas: "Prudence is the best part of courage, and it is in any case a requirement of responsibility" (1990 [1979], 257).

This search for a type of governance adapted to the "uncertain world" (Callon et al. 2001) does not imply that one agrees with the way the precautionary principle must be applied. Is it necessary to retain the most extreme scenarios when one tries to evaluate the gravity of a danger? By overly preaching prudence, doesn't one end up promoting the idea that zero risk could exist? As has been shown by Callon and his colleagues, the texts produced within the national framework or by international authorities, such as the Convention of Rio or the European Commission, diverge, as much regarding the manner of evaluating the threshold from which the precautionary principle must apply, as regarding the optional or constraining character of the entrance into precaution. They also differ on the extent of the measures to be implemented: is precaution just synonymous with abstention, or does it imply specific initiatives?

The fact that the policy leaves jurisdictions to define the issue for themselves is also significant: on the GMO issue, it was the State Council which, in France, at the request of Greenpeace, deferred the request to execute the decree of 5 May 1998 authorizing the transgenic culture of corn. Is this to say that the rise in power of the concept of precaution would be synonymous with a relative withdrawal of politics, in a field where scientists on one side and jurists on the other now pull the strings? As the jurist Marie-Angèle Hermitte indicates, in connection with the controversies on the patentability of living beings and the therapeutic cloning of the human embryos, it should not thus be concluded that politics has become destitute. "Science, taking note of its uncertainty, returns all its autonomy to politics. . . . In such situations it is for politicians to define the level of acceptable risk and especially the type of risk that society wants to run" (2001, 48). In other words, the ball is in the political court, and it is there that public opinion awaits it. So much so that *it* can be directly attacked, as *it* was in the case of the contaminated blood affair, in which the French prime minister and the minister of health were blamed directly. The issue raised was precisely that of the *responsibility* of leaders, and we still remember the devastating effects of the expression of one of their colleagues—"responsible, but not guilty"—which durably symbolized the offhanded attitude of politicians.

It is, moreover, a question that arises often in relation to those who exert power in our society. Are they really able to confront these problems, to project themselves out of their own routines in order to face the threats that weigh on the future? For we are no longer waiting for them to announce the brilliance that tomorrow will bring. In the same way, their announcements of reforms no longer succeed in convincing the public. In the survival perspective, the anticipation of a negative reaction has now become essential. In this new dialectic, being positive is not important (one remembers the sad fate that befell Jean-Pierre Raffarin, the former French prime minister, when he sang of a "positive attitude"). What matters now is to appear permanently disquiet, faced with every form of threat. To govern in a space of uncertainty: this is what people ask of their elected officials. When the latter pretend to get rid of threats, they are exposed to a reaction that sometimes stupefies them, as the referendum on the European constitution illustrated.

On this occasion a real gap grew between the political leaders and the majority of French and other European citizens. Nothing seemed to predict the result of this vote. No political scientist would have forecasted that it would start such a mobilization of opinion. Yet, not only was the debate intense, but, on the day of the vote, the voters turned out in mass. They called for a definitive No. But what precisely was the issue? The constitutional treaty to be ratified or rejected was a complex text, presenting both a charter of basic rights, a reform of the organization of powers within the EU, and a statement of the various public policies installed within this framework. Thick, sometimes esoteric, the constitution nonetheless polarized the interests of the French, as the publishing success of the various books—explanatory and critical—that were devoted to the issue demonstrates. On the podium and in the media, the polemic raged. Even better: we witnessed the hatching of an incredible number of websites, and internet users were particularly verbose. All of this just to lead to a definitive No which left the deaf European elites stupefied. Months later we still wondered about the significance of this event.

In the perspective of its authors and partisans, the constitution incarnated an opening toward the future. It offered the possibility to reinforce Europe, to make it into a real political power, able to confront the United States and China in the context of a merciless economic competition, and to challenge the hegemonic claims of American leaders. From a rational point of view, the constitution presented an unquestionable positivity. It carried in it an entirety of unsolved problems, causing, among other things, interrogations on the future of the French "social model" within a more and more integrated economic ensemble.

Without returning to the arguments of the partisans and adversaries of the referendum, we can try to interpret the victory of its rejection in light of the preceding considerations. The explanations given generally take one of two paths. The first regards French domestic policy, in which the No is considered as the expression of a generalized dissatisfaction and the rejection of the current government. In this perspective, Europe was taken hostage, and people responded negatively to a question that had not been asked. The other path takes the European motivations of voters seriously, who in this case expressed their disapproval in regard to the consequences of both widening the EU and the EU constitution's neoliberal slant. Obviously, each of the two explanations makes up part of the truth; in the speeches given by the treaty's adversaries, domestic politics and the opposition to a Europe exclusively dedicated to the market were quite present. If we add the "sovereignist" layer,[1] we obtain a rather faithful spectrum of the No, broad enough to perturb on the left as well as on the right.

Must we leave it at that? I believe that doing so would be to lose sight of a specific dimension of the May 29, 2005, vote. It undoubtedly produced a phenomenon of great breadth, which any type of explanation taking into account just the question/answer sequence can reflect only imperfectly. The vote was clearly an answer to the question asked, whether it concerned a response to the constitution's legitimacy or a response that shifted the legitimacy issue to those who raised the question. But we can also wonder whether the No suggested a pressing examination of the way that politics treats the future. As if once again citizens were confronted with

1. The sovereignist voters see Europe as a threat for national independence and they are against the idea of a European government. For them, more political integration is synonymous with a loss of national sovereignty.

a programmatic engagement, in itself coherent, but which ignored the essential, with this space of uncertainty looming in the wake of European construction. We have emphasized to what point Europe, as an unidentified political object, was linked to the virtual, as a mechanism that never stops projecting itself into the future. This inclination results in its powerful and disquieting character. It is not by chance that each stage of European construction generates, at some time or another, these reactions of rejection. However, by illustrating the possibility of an acceleration of the integration process, the constitution reopened Pandora's box. It is important to mention the debates that raged between the two camps: at each confrontation we witnessed a quasi-analogue scene where the constitution's flatterers conscientiously enumerated its assets and projections as its opponents pointed to all the faults in its structure. So much so that the prevailing feeling—undoubtedly related to the programmatic character of the text—was that something important was missing, something which would have made this constitution an instrument both essential and impossible to circumvent.

While seeking to give an account of this strange frustration, one realizes that it is the will to take into account the multiple implications of European construction which ended up producing ambivalent—or quite simply ambiguous—formulations. The fact that the text results from a compromise between disparate approaches could only reinforce this feeling of artificiality. By wanting to be complete, one attracted the curiosity of the public toward the zones of the unsaid, causing uncertainty. My hypothesis is that this uncertainty itself ended up generating a reaction of precaution. As one commentator observes: "The 'No' camp succeeded in imposing its set of themes based on social insecurity, worsened by an unreassuring European future" (Dupin 2005).[2] What seems to prevail in public opinion, in particular on the left, is the idea of a diffuse threat which can take a caricatured form, such as when the image of the Polish plumber was used to "represent" the threat of unemployment.

Confronted with the unknown, the reflex consists not in abstaining from a decision but in taking initiative. There is certainly no scientific proof that the European constitution is a vector of danger. Similarly, we cannot rigorously demonstrate the causal link between beef consumption contaminated by animal flours and Creutzfeldt-Jakob disease. But vigilance is essential: just as we destroy whole herds likely to be infected, we also reject a text whose supposed consequences are potentially negative, without encountering any opposition. It is revealing that the Yes camp also employed the argument of the lesser of two evils in support of its position: only a politically strong Europe would be capable of limiting the damage that globalization could bring.

The French No to the referendum of May 2005 can thus be described as a vote of precaution. Like the principle of the same name, it is based on a consideration of the nega-

2. Dupin adds, "We made a mistake in thinking that this referendum was made into a 'sanction-vote' against an unpopular executive. The unhappiness of French people is more profound than this, anchored in social distrust itself coupled to European stakes" (*Les Echos* 2005).

tive consequences of the action likely to be undertaken. In Aristotelian terms, we get a syllogism of this sort: "If I vote yes, there is a risk of negative consequences; however, any negative consequence must be avoided; thus I do not vote for this text." What is interesting in this reaction is not that it clarifies the gravity of the problems faced by the French regarding employment. After all, this situation is not new. If there is any innovation, it concerns the voters' attitude and their way of contrasting prudence to the unknown. Perhaps the No is nothing more than the political expression of the Responsibility Principle, dear to the philosopher Hans Jonas. Democracy now functions on the horizon of survival; the implicit mandate entrusted by citizens to their representatives consists in controlling the risks induced by political action as much as possible. In this context, any initiative likely to cause turbulence appears inopportune and can only meet the disavowal of the governed. The personalization of votes is no longer successful; voters now expect that candidates will emphasize the horizon of negativity on which any political action is sure to unfold, and that they will show their aptitude to face the threatening future thanks to some proposals illustrating the ethics of responsibility.

It is interesting to compare what occurred in 2005 with "the strange defeat" of presidential candidate Lionel Jospin three years before: hypermobilization on one side, abstentionism and a scattering of votes in the first electoral round on the other. The contrast between voters' behaviors seems blinding, so much so that certain observers saw in the voter turnout of 2005 a true citizen jolt in reaction to political inertia, a jolt which propelled Jean-Marie Le Pen to the presidential final. There are still issues to be raised: after all, isn't the apparent absence of voter motivation in 2002 registered in the same logic as the passion expressed for the European vote? A simple flashback on the presidential campaign allows us to remember that the only topic which caused a stir at the time was insecurity. The expected debate on social and economic issues was from the start relegated to the background. The question was not whether Jospin's program was socialist or not, or if Chirac represented the interests of big business owners. The major concern related to insecurity and the means of confronting it. It is no surprise that the speeches placing threat in the foreground incited support. At the same time, it would be too hasty to attribute the election result to the pervasiveness of an "ideology of security."

Public opinion is indeed polarized over the problems related to delinquency and the various forms of incivility, but such concerns are above all part of a broad portrayal of the diffuse and permanent threat to our societies. Without any doubt the events of September 11, 2001, were a factor in the intertwining of risk and collective choices. But as we saw, many other ingredients come into play in this representation. What is new is not so much that humans feel weakened because of the expansion of knowledge and technology, with the harmful effects that they bring and the potentiality of collecting these capacities for purely destructive ends. The theme of the sorcerer's apprentice, from Prometheus to Frankenstein, has haunted our senses for quite some time. *The new aspect resides in the clash between the problems of the polis and those of survival*. In this respect, April 2002 and May 2005 represent two possible answers. In the first case, disinterest clings to the idea that the essential aspects of survival did not enter into this combat, personalized to the extreme: there was the prescience that the true stakes escaped the nation-state configuration, which none of the presidential challengers was able to recognize. At the time of the referendum, the horizon of survival was omnipresent, and the extent of the debate signifies the displacement which took place. With the rejection of the referendum arose both a true effort to attach oneself to territory's traditional dimension, as well as a process which projects us toward a globality experienced as a threat.

So that I am understood: this is not a question of measuring or evaluating the result of a democratic process, of which historians of centuries to come will be better able to measure the consequences. Whether the Yes or No won out in the end, what matters is the cognitive configuration that animated the controversy and the passions that it triggered. One can, on the contrary, try to get some distance in order to better measure how the entanglement of politics and survival constitutes an innovation in the functioning of societies. With this intention, I propose a detour to distant regions and a confrontation with different experiences.

A nthropologists have written extensively about the forms of societal organization, all of which contributes today to show the inanity of the adjective "primitive" for which they were ridiculed. Thanks to the considerable work achieved by several generations of researchers in very diverse fields, we know a little more about the manners of living in society that contrast with the standards imposed by modernity. It is necessary, however, to point to a certain ambiguity: while ethnographers have certainly allowed us to discover systems very different from our own, they have also revealed the universality of certain questions, even if the answers societies produce can diverge considerably. In particular, this is the case regarding the need to establish some form of government.

As the renowned comparatist A. M. Hocart observed, "We shall see all the functions of the government discharged among the people without government . . . without our being able to point to any particular body of men regulating social intercourse" (1970 [1936], 30). This is the same as saying that politics is there even if there is no specialized body that deals with common affairs. There are several examples of this situation, beginning with the Nuer of Sudan described by E. E. Evans-Pritchard (1966 [1940]), among whom one finds neither an authority, strictly speaking, nor any form of coordination. The Nuer represent the ideal-type of a headless society. That does not imply, however, that there is no political organization. Evans-Pritchard identifies tribes that each include several thousands of people. The individuals whom he met, moreover, had a clear awareness of their tribal

membership. The tribe is the most extended community within which a disagreement can be regulated by arbitration, whereas an opposing litigation from members of different tribes is likely to generate a war. The Nuer have neither institutions nor political authority. We would be more likely to designate, with Evans-Pritchard, their "political values." Regarding the "political system," it is above all a balance between the opposed tendencies of fission and fusion. In any case, in this population as in other African groups known as "segmentary societies," such as the Tallensi, the specific absence of governmental equipment does not imply the inexistence of a form of governmentality.

Should we conclude, with Hocart, that even in the communities that seem to be the most distant from our political constructs, "the machinery of government is there, ready to govern, if governing is required. There is, so to speak, a governing body before there is any governing to do" (1970 [1936], 31). This line of reasoning seems like a sort of arbitrary presupposition: either the need for this kind of organizational form arises and so it actually comes into existence; or this need does not arise, and as a result the organism in question remains in the fictive domain. In one case, we have a tautology, and, in the other, a pure contradiction. What does Hocart mean by this paradoxical statement? In fact, our author is associating two distinct concepts, that of government and that of ritual. This association is what gives meaning to his attempt to consider the universality of politics through the assertion of the existence of a governmental organism—to some extent virtual—always already co-present with society. Well before the emergence of governmental forms, there is the implementation of "ritual organization," intended for the achievement of acts concerning the relationship that humans maintain with life. It is initially this ritual organization that provides the functions of governmentality; only later does political organization in its specificity appear, next to the ritual apparatus.

To account for the genesis of any government, it is thus necessary to take the precedence of ritual into account. Ritual, however, only makes sense because ritual maintains a specific relation with life. "To understand the oldest role that we know of this [governmental] apparatus, we must study the idea of life that man has" (Hocart 1970 [1936], 31). Everything is thus tied to the problematic of life, starting from an interrogation that Hocart summarizes as follows: "If life comes and goes, it is necessary that it comes from somewhere and goes somewhere" (1970 [1936], 32); hence the effort humans give to understanding this coming-and-going and to controlling it. They thus invent a set of processes containing gestures and words. This is what anthropologists indicate under the name of ritual. "Everywhere, men pronounce formulas and achieve ritual acts with the intention to move life from one object to another" (ibid.). Anthropologists have often stressed that at the origin of the practices and beliefs generally included under the categories of ritual, magic, and religion is the question of the relationship to nature, that is, the mysterious powers that man endeavors to domesticate. The very possibility of surviving within a threatening universe — of ensuring life's perpetuation and of understanding the way life is transmitted and circulates between beings — is in question. It is no surprise that those in charge of ritual functions are also invested with a particular power with regard to society. The political organization emerged as such through a progressive process of differentiation and specification. But it was born from "an undifferentiated organization intended to promote life."

In the beginning, social order and the natural order overlapped so narrowly that one can consider the relationship to existence to have been constitutive of the relationship to power. In Amazonian societies, persons such as shamans, intercessors between human and supernatural powers, incarnate this confluence of power, life force, and guarantee of a social order. They play the part of doctors of bodies and souls, and initiate the important collective activities such as hunting and war. Another characteristic phenomenon studied by anthropologists is divine royalty. In his famous work *The Golden Bough*, James Frazer (1925) qualifies Divine Kingship as the institution where the leaders not only are equipped with supernatural powers, such as rainmaking, soothsaying, sorcery, and healing, but are also so completely identified with nature and the harvest cycle that they were killed in the event of a natural disaster (such as droughts and epidemics) or when judged too weakened or old (see also Richards 1968).

The divine king is the power of life; he is identified with life, and *his* life accounts for the survival of his people. This institution is based on a set of beliefs that attribute to the divine king a power over nature, which he exercises voluntarily or involuntarily, and it makes him the dynamic center of the universe so that his actions and even the course of his life affect its wellbeing. Thus he must be permanently under control because his absolute power carries the danger of disorder; he can involve the whole world in his own decline. The ritual murder of the sovereign, when his forces decrease, constitutes the best means "of ensuring that the fall of the God-man does not involve the fall of the world" (Seligman 1934, 4).

Among the Jukun (see Young 1966; Meek 1931), a society in northern Nigeria, the *Aku*—as the king was called—was metaphorically associated with the sun and the moon. The Aku was simultaneously the supreme chief, the rainmaker, and the protector of grain. The ear of wheat, the clothing of the rainmaker, and the whip of coercion were the symbols of his power. The principal aspect of his might—this spiritual force which is the quintessence of royalty—was indicated by a specific term: *juwe*. Michael W. Young sees the equivalent of juwe in the *dignitas* analyzed in connection with English royalty by the historian Ernst Kantorowicz. This force was immortal and inviolable. It was localized in the heart and the right arm of the Aku. His people also gave the new king his predecessor's powdered heart to eat, and he had to keep his predecessor's arm as a sacred relic.

Innumerable taboos surrounded the sovereign because his power was dangerous, and such taboos were essential to the protection of his subjects. Any contact with him implied a fatal contamination. Among the most important ordeals is an oath made by touching the king's bed. If he lied, the individual was struck down and died immediately. The rites practiced by Aku were made to bring wellbeing to his people. It was not enough that the sovereign existed; his role was to maintain harmony between society and its natural environment. According to the tradition, the Aku was put to death after he had reigned for seven years. But he could also be put to death in the case of a famine, if he fell from a horse, or in the event of the transgression of royal taboos. Similarly, he was executed if he became very sick. He was secretly strangled.

The life of the king was completely identified with the life of harvests. When he appeared in public, he was welcomed by his subjects, prostrate in front of him and crying, "Our harvests! Our wheat! Our beans! Our nuts! Our rain! Our richness! Our health!" The grain of the royal farm was used to make sacred beer that the sovereign consumed daily. By drinking, he communed with the gods and ancestors immanent in him. It was said that if the king were buried during the dry season, harvests would disappear with him, that they "would have died" with him. The sovereign was foremost a "corn-king," so much so that we can wonder whether the periodicity of the ritual regicide can be explained by the recurrence of famines in this area, the king thus functioning as a scapegoat whose execution was likely to restore the harmony of the natural cycle. It was also the means for humans to affirm their influence over nature and their control of the absolute power incarnated in a figure whose destiny was to ensure the survival of the world and the society at the price of his own life.

In the Africanist literature, Aku Jukun is not an isolated case; among others, we can cite the *Mukama* of Bunyoro and the *Mugabe* of Ankole (Uganda), the *Reth* of Shilluk (Sudan), the *Utu* of the Rukuba and the *Alafin* of Oyo (Nigeria), the *Lwembe* of Nyakusa (Tanzania), and the *Oba* of Benin, all of whom are invested with supernatural powers and also destined to meet an unfortunate end. Beyond the diversity of areas and situations, what is striking is the overlapping of politics and survival. Among the Nyakusa, the Lwembe was seen as the ensurer of growth, rain, food, milk, and the birth of children. In another context, regarding the Moundang of Chad, Alfred Adler (1982) underlines the extraordinary intimacy between sovereign and the natural cycle: "The study of the calendar and the various ceremonial cycles undeniably illustrated that the king of Léré is most intimately associated with the cycle of vegetation—both as its most important sacrifice and as a body transformed through sacrament. His *ké*, his magic power to cause or prevent rainfall, his capacity to provoke disasters and various calamities against the population, attributed to him by the Moundang, make him the person in charge of climatic hazards" (393).

About the Oba of Benin, it was said that "the king is like the day, he gives his food to the day" (Bradbury 1967). Among the Bemba, kings prayed for peace, for luck, and for their subjects to be protected from accidents. They also needed to perform rituals that preceded the annual cutting of trees and initiated the cycle of economic activities. It was said that they thus "heated" their territory. The choice of metaphors is significant. Among the Nyoro, the death of the Mukama was announced by the cry: "The goblet of milk is broken" (Roscoe 1968; see also Beattie 1959). Like the Jukun sovereign, the Mukama is equipped with a supernatural power, the *mahano*. This force symbolizes both authority and the spiritual dimension of power. It is placed in the body of the king and is concretized by the eruption of unforeseeable violence. In several studies, we find the same dangerousness of a force that can be a factor of disorder. The subjects of the Mukama fear and respect the mahano.

In divine kingship, sovereignty is associated with hubris and transgression. The monarch carries in his being all the power of life, and he is also the guarantor of the universe's durability. We are dealing with a founding imbalance that confronts men with a contradiction which this institution seems programmed to control. If we look more closely, the monstrosity of the royal figure is due to the fact that it functions in all its power precisely because it is not delimited only by the cultural codes governing the group. All the ethnographic descriptions highlight the radical uncertainty of divine kingship, at the junction of nature and culture. Anthropologists have illustrated how certain primordial prohibitions are transgressed; to start with, incest—which Lévi-Strauss showed to mark the passage between nature and culture. "Kings and sorcerers, the Bushong say, do not know shame. They live beyond society" (Vansina 1954). The existence of matrimonial relationships, of consummated or symbolic unions between close relatives, is manifested in 133 the majority of the divine kingships. Among the Ankole of Uganda, where the *bahima* pastoralists dominated the *bahirou* farmers, the sovereign was associated with his mother and his sister, and both had practically the same status as the king himself. It seems that in Bantou societies, incest was truly and ritually consummated. The king Lunda sanctioned his union with his sister with one gesture: raising her skirt, he looked at her genitals. The case of the Luba society, whose king had sexual relations with his mother, is even more significant.

There are many other testimonies of royal incest. It is thus traditional among the Lozi of Rhodesia that incest is achieved between the king and his half sister. Among the Lele of Kasaï, incest is an essential element of the enthronement ritual. Mary Douglas points out that it is a major crime, matched only by intraclan murder in its seriousness. However, the future chief is supposed to kill a clan brother at each rite of passage of his adolescence. According to the anthropologist, these two types of transgression (incest and murder of a clan brother) are precisely regarded as the source of magic power (Douglas 1963, 202). They are, nonetheless, two crimes that connect man to animals.

Luc de Heusch (1958) has also mentioned the "sociologically incestuous character" of these unions. The violation of exogamic constraints imposes a double rule. These diverse forms of royal incest—since certain kings marry (but without necessarily consummating the marriage) uterine sisters, half sisters, or even another close relative prohibited in common unions—illustrate the sovereign's obligation, on the one hand, to marry outside of ordinary practices, and on the other hand to challenge the matrimonial standards which apply to the members of his own clan. The intrinsic assertion of transgression is a manifestation of the autonomy of power. The king appears to be freed from any dependence on the community. He is located beyond the exogamic stakes, "out of the circuit of matrimonial alliances that found vulgar society" (1958). By short-circuiting the exogamic processes, the royalty designates its holder as existing outside of the clan. Most significant of the theoretical developments on divine kingship is perhaps the double maxim of the Swazi, observing on the one hand that "the king is a king from his people" and on the other hand that "the king is not followed" (the brothers born after him are not his true brothers).

In representations of divine kingship, an act which constitutes a strict transgression from the point of view of cultural codes endows the sovereign with absolute power. By acting like an animal,[1] he is no longer simply one with nature—he incarnates the very quintessence of life. The same societies which condemn any attack on exogamic principles nevertheless welcome the regenerating and fertilizing virtues of the incestuous union. The cow given to the king by his incestuous wife is, among the Nyoro, the positive symbol of this situation. Bestiality, monstrosity, it does not matter! We see here a *supplement* that neither nature nor culture alone is able to obtain for humans. The supreme power carries excess within itself; it is like a life flux that relentlessly feeds the world. It is thus necessary that this life power is deployed at the heart of society. As in many monarchies of this type, the Moundang see a true microcosm in the royal palace, and king of the Léré is compared to the sun that lights this universe. "He rotates around the sacred enclosure that his wives occupy, whom he took from the four corners of the Moundang country," notes Adler (1982, 314).

The image of this monarch who rotates like the sun inside his palace is particularly striking. It is as though the flux was domesticated, as though the impossible junction of nature and culture was carried out in a circumscribed space and under society's control. It is not true that the threat superpower brings to the divine king is impossible to neutralize. Because this is the central dilemma: if one assumes, as do his

1. Other customs underline the animal side of sovereignty, such as the custom of offering a basket full of rats to the Bushong king during his sacrament, whereas these rodents profoundly disgust his people (see Vansina 1955).

contemporaries, that the sovereign must enjoy his absolute power and that any mark of weakness is harmful, it is necessary to respect — even if one fears it more than anything — this singular quality of the unique being dedicated to ensuring the junction of culture and nature, and, beyond that, of living conditions and survival. At the same time, controlling this power is important, and this is the function of the taboos surrounding the monarch. These taboos result in the Jukun paradox: it is because the Aku is a corn king that he is not allowed to visit the wheat fields; by approaching them, he risks devastating the harvests. Everywhere in the divine kingships, there is a barrage of taboos that *a contrario* highlight the virtually negative impact of absolute power. Among the Moundang, the king of Léré must not be seen eating and he must not trample the ground with his bare foot. He can neither urinate nor defecate without a slave collecting these dangerous excretions (Adler 1982, 314). Both articulated and tacit, a set of proscriptions regulates the relationship between the king and his subjects. These proscriptions form more than a simple protocol because by transgressing certain rules, one risks his life.

The constraints of this avoidance outline a potential danger and isolate not only the person but also the royal position from the remainder of the society. The consubstantial excess of sovereignty is this "beyond" of bare life that produces the universe. But the "cultured" individual must never be confronted with this excess, or he will undergo the destructive effects of the absolute power on which his destiny depends. Nothing is more essential than superpower, and yet nothing is more dangerous. That the superpower is not held back must be ensured, while its potentially harmful effects also have to be controlled. This ambivalence is strongly expressed in certain rituals, such as the annual ceremonies of Incwala practiced by the Swazi, where the contradictory effects of divine kingship are staged. At the exact moment when the king will be regenerated and show his absolute power as the country's true "bull," the Swazi sing, You hate the king! Royalty is intolerable! The reign comes to an end in these songs of pain and of mourning, showing the ambiguity of the relation between the people and their sovereign; the enemies are neither interior troublemakers nor the foreign attackers, but all Swazi. They are the same ones who will applaud the regeneration of the king, after driving out the real foreigners and the dominating clan: this is the first phase of the social reappropriation of power. The second phase, corresponding to the great day of Incwala, begins with songs of pain: the king did not die; the king is naked.

Everything begins anew. "The work of the king is quite heavy," as an old Swazi man said. But as soon as the king forms a unit with the nation, to which he transmits his power, the members of the royal clan react. Inviting him to leave the country, they seek to regain their sovereignty, by moving their relative away from his people. Hilda Kuper proposes two interpretations: either the royal clan wants to take the king and to leave their country; or, on the contrary, the royal clan provokes the king and shouts its hatred. The songs and the dances are indeed ambiguous: on the one hand, the clan encircles the king, omnipresent as during the sovereign's entire existence; on the other hand, the king escapes his clan; it is the illusion of sovereignty, the almighty's seizing of the dominating clan's power. It is like a seesaw: the excluded dominating clan yields their place; it is the people's turn to control their king. At this point, there is the last symbolic inversion; by throwing them a gourd, the king returns the ball to their court (see Kuper 1947).

These comings-and-goings, this back-and-forth game that stages the king, his close relations, and his people, translate—in an extremely elaborate mise-en-scène—the complex relationships of force that set up the royalty and the constituents of society. Absolute power can be neither hailed nor tamed. It escapes the clan from which it results, but cannot be controlled by the people. This does not prevent society from placing it under surveillance, to avoid its excesses, and especially to be ready to replace the sovereign at the smallest sign of failure. Nothing less than the survival of men and their world is at stake, so it is essential that the king never dies. The ritual regicide undoubtedly seemed the surest means to prevent "the world [from being] damaged along with him," according to a formula of the Anyi of Ivory Coast (see Perrot 1982). It is the surest means of controlling absolute power. Must we thus conclude, along with Michael W. Young, that "in periodically killing one who transcends nature by controlling it and transcends society by embodying it, men assert their command over nature and their final control of society"(1966, 151)? It seems, rather, that the beliefs connected to the murder of the king strongly express the difficulty that societies undergo when confronting the all-powerful as well as the tensions that result from this confrontation.

It is no surprise that the periods of interregnum are particularly favorable to all kinds of disorders. In these situations, it is important to prevent anarchy at all costs and to avoid any loss of absolute power. So that "the king never dies," among the Suku of Zaire, a human-sized mannequin, wearing the king's insignia, takes the place of the late king (Balandier 1985, 38). It is to the mannequin that notables come to present their condolences and to offer their funerary gifts. The transitional phase ends with the enthronement **139** of the new king and the accession of the old one to the rank of royal ancestor. Another manner of controlling the threat of anarchy in the interregnums is to pantomime it in order to better suppress it. Thus the grand rituals of inversion proceed, during which the captives seize the royal insignia and do not hesitate to deride the established order. The comedy does not last long, and everything is put back in order with the beginning of a new reign.

What matters most of all is to ensure the transmission of force without the universe plunging into darkness, hence the extreme precision of the rites through which the transfer of certain force-carrying organs to the new sovereign takes place. Many divine kings ingest these organs (such as the Alafin Oyo and Aku Jukun who eat the heart of their predecessor reduced to powder, or the Utu Rukuba who drinks beer containing parts of his predecessor's skull), while others preserve them in a safe place (the king of Léré preciously keeps the skull of his predecessor, which then serves as one of his instruments of power).

This configuration of practices and beliefs condensed in the politico-ritual device of divine kingship illustrates the centrality of the problems of survival. Through a sometimes very sophisticated symbolism that simultaneously involves human, nonhuman, and superhuman actors, a figure of superpower is concretized as the guarantor of the group's reproduction and development in a threatening environment. We have often pontificated about the symbolic and ritual dimensions of the phenomenon. Although the use of the concepts of sacredness and divinity does justice to the explicitly supernatural character of sovereignty, such concepts are nevertheless heavy with religious connotations, risking the authorization of sometimes superficial connections to Western traditions of divine-right monarchies. The categories of transcendence and the hereafter, however, seem poorly disposed to the analysis of this mechanism.

The "divine" or "miracle-worker" king is foremost the product of a representation that focuses on the concept of superpower, concentrated in sovereignty, and temporarily belongs to the being in charge of it. There is no necessary reference to gods in this case, unlike doctrines that make them the indispensable origin of all power. Superpower is an end in itself because it achieves the junction of nature and culture by producing this continuous flow of life essential to the regeneration of the world. "Sovereignty finds its base in an image of the world, it secretes . . . a kind of microcosm, referee and guarantor of the union of man and universe" (Adler 1982,

398). I will suggest that the originality of this system relies on what society produces in a permanent dialectic with this representation of superpower.

From this point of view, the question of survival receives a particularly refined treatment. Not only does the reality of superpower, attested to by the sovereign's own hubris, constitute in itself the guarantee of the universe's reproduction, but, moreover, humans control how the kingship is exercised, thus giving themselves the means to control of their future. This is the process that produces power relations; it is the origin of politics. Superpower is in some sense the exterior through which society is reflected and defined, to borrow the terms employed by the philosopher Claude Lefort concerning power (1986, 265). *This presence of superpower in society is the first element through which the relationships that we generally designate as political are put into place, whether they deal with cooperation or subordination. We can see here the strong overlap between politics and survival in a mechanism where the dimension of power over men seems to come second—it is in the domain of the relative compared to the absolute of superpower. This configuration is thoroughly ordered by the problematic of survival. That which comes from harmoniously living together (convivance), such as societal organization and its hierarchies, is entirely subordinated to the implementation of a dynamic of life and survival.* In the figure of the divine king, superpower incarnates the guarantee of life and survival against any attack.

Although the royal function plays a central role in the assurance of the world's continuation, he who assumes this role is placed under the sign of precariousness. "His passion for survival, which might otherwise grow to dangerous proportions during the course of his reign, is blunted and checked from the very start. The king knows when he will die, and this is sooner than many of his subjects. He is a ruler who, in accepting the office, renounces the despot's claim to survive at all costs," observes Canetti (1984 [1962], 418). The sovereign incarnates the conditions of world survival. He is in charge of the goal of collective survival, but his own mortal nature only ensures a precarious status for him, hence the proposed assimilation between the divine king and the figure of the scapegoat (see Muller 1980). It is the sovereign's vocation to offer, constrained and forced, his own life in exchange for the regeneration of the universe. In this system, superpower has, as a counterpart, the precariousness of power over men—the latter no more than an attribute derived from the former. The representation that underlies this figure of sovereignty has the double interest of registering the political on the horizon of survival and managing a disjunction between superpower and power, with the latter permanently subjected to the control of the group.

6 From Power to Humanity

I f we now turn to contemporary societies, we realize the extent to which the situation is different. In our democracies, where the problem of convivance has imposed itself over the last several centuries, we have few tools to consider politics on the horizon of survival. On the other hand, the sphere of power has not stopped inflating. It is even necessary to speak of a "political bubble," making an analogy with the expression that bloomed in the field of finance. The political bubble is often assimilated to the omnipotent, even ventripotent state: by integrating new functions of social protection, the modern state took on a considerable weight. Generally, criticisms regarding the political bubble were aimed at the state. The state is not only used as a tried and true concept; it is often seen as a convenient metaphor to signify this inflation of power that appears to the multitude as disconnected from its aspirations. There is indeed an ensemble of discourses centered on the denunciation and criticism of state dysfunctions and excesses. The fact that one rails against the bureaucracy is nothing new, and neither are the attacks that take aim at the various forms of coercion exercised by the administration. The criticism of power, insofar as power is incarnated in the state and its leaders, has generally led to two positions. On the one hand, there is the anarchistic critic who wants to be the expression of the society against the state and aims at dismantling the political leviathan by all means necessary. On the other hand, we have the Marxist critic who encourages, in a transitional phrase, the reappropriation of the state by the dominated class (the dictatorship of the proletariat) in order to lead to its progressive extinction within the framework of a classless society.

It must be recognized that, as virulent as they are, these two modes of denunciation jointly fall under the prospect for a better world. Both kinds of struggles must permit the abolition of any obstacle to the realization of a society organized around wisdom and happiness. Proudhon and Marx each want to be, in their own way, the architects and developers in the service of a positive utopia. Furthermore, these doctrines are placed under the Hope Principle.[1] This principle can function within these theories because the societal evils to be remedied are part of a history marked by the passage from feudalism to capitalism, which occurred by the imposition of a mode of production based on the extortion of surplus value, which in turn has transformed a growing number of human beings into workers exploited by a minority. As Marx insists, however, this history does not merge with a destiny in

1. According to the expression of philosopher Ernest Bloch.

which it would be forever impossible to be freed. Admittedly, it produces an organization of society that alienates the great mass of producers. And yet, the knowledge of the causes of this alienation should make it possible to put the world on its feet and promote the conditions of the emancipation of the masses.

In this schema, everything is played out within the dialectic of the political and the social, on the horizon of rationality that is likely to improve the lot of humanity while acting on the contradictions of capitalism. The twentieth century showed the limits of this "progressivist" aim. It is not my intention to broach either the assessment of "real socialism" or the controversies about the responsibility of Marxism and Leninism for the derivatives of the experiments to which they gave birth. What interests me more particularly is that we are located in a demiurgic vision where it is foremost a question of constructing a society that assigns work, politics, and culture their specific places.

There is, strictly speaking, nothing *beyond* society. In this conception, in contrast to the representation at work in divine kingship, the problems of survival are totally absent. The reproduction of the world takes place in ways shaped entirely by the society: "I am the master of myself as I am the master of the universe"; thus men seem to themselves in the framework of progressive rationalism.

There is, however, a whole side of recent history that collides with the logic of convivance, concerning the state and the dialectic between power and society. Hannah Arendt showed how, in the interwar period, a category of "the rightless" emerged, with refugees and stateless people resulting from the collapse of the Russian, Austro-Hungarian, and Ottoman empires—hence the surge of White Russians, Armenians, Bulgarians, Greeks, Hungarians, and Romanians on the European scene. All these people lost not only their social and cultural bonds of origin, but also the political protection that a government can offer. No longer having a place in a community, being deprived of political status, they "lack that tremendous equalizing of differences which comes from being citizens of some commonwealth and yet, since they are no longer allowed to partake in the human artifice, they begin to belong to the human race in much the same way as animals belong to a specific animal species" (Arendt 1973, 286). Going even further, it restores the terrifying process at the end of which, deprived of his legal self, amputated from his moral self, the "rightless" is only left with disappearing purely and simply: "The one thing that still prevents men from being made into living corpses is the differentiation of the individual, his unique identity" (Arendt 1968, 149). When Arendt speaks to us about the Holocaust, she clarifies the *political* assumptions of the genocide—the way that state power can transform humans into a species of men who "have lost precisely those qualities that make it possible for others to treat them as fellow human beings" (1973, 286).

During these last thirty years, this issue of "the questioning of the human quality [that] causes a quasi-biological claim of belonging to the human race" (Antelme 1998 [1957], 25) has always been on the agenda. That we could legally and according to industrial methods proceed with the destruction of whole peoples raises not only the question of systematic state terror. It also implies that a power assumes the right "to determine who should and who should not inhabit the world" (Arendt 1992 [1963], 279). As Arendt sees it, the idea of politics is faced with the complex question of radical evil. Whereas the Moderns were never able to contend with the strictly ethical stakes of political action, after the Holocaust it became impossible to disregard this dimension of problems. Or, to be more precise, the human question comes to haunt consciences and captivates us in our approach to world events. It is in this context that organizations defined 147 as nongovernmental affirm themselves and, beginning in the 1970s, intervene in the Third World. Massive displacements of populations and the multiplication of refugee camps: this situation constituted a favorable context for the development of organizations such as Doctors without Borders, Action against Hunger, and Handicap International. In addition to the immediate assistance that these organizations are able to provide, they also have a function of testimony and information with regard to the international community, denouncing breaches of human rights.

The rise in power of humanitarian organizations and the echo that their action experienced in Western populations constitutes without any doubt one of the remarkable occurrences of the last thirty years. In their wake, a whole constellation of NGOs has been created, exerting their competences in very diverse fields. But it is no coincidence if we spontaneously include this type of sociopolitical actor in a category with rather vague contours: *the humanitarian*. The multiplication of the occurrences of this adjective is significant: one speaks about humanitarian engagement, humanitarian emergency, and even of humanitarian philosophy. Regarding this last one, Rony Brauman, who directed Doctors without Borders between 1982 and 1994, gives the following definition: "Deep down, the man who aims for humane principles is not the 'political animal,' but a negatively defined being; to the question 'What is man?' humane philosophy answers simply that he is not made to suffer. Humane principles prohibit thinking about suffering in regard to history and politics" (2002 [1996], 48). This assumed separation between the humanitarian and the political opens up a space of action and communication for NGOs, incomparable to the space they had occupied until that time. It is now their role to deal with the problems of survival, which grants them a strong legitimacy among a public increasingly sensitive to the question of human rights and more and more skeptical of the power (and the will) of governments to ensure the universal application of such principles.

NGOs will progressively disturb the routines of the democracy of indifference and will prove their capacity to cause mobilizations of solidarity concerning political powers and institutions. Amnesty International launches large campaigns against Latin American dictatorships. In Western democracies, campaigns in favor of humanitarian aid have extensive media coverage. The intolerable character of the spectacle of famine, in contexts where humans seem abandoned by powers and institutions, now unsettles the agendas of great powers by impelling the redevelopment of their priorities. We are witnessing the constitution of a new cause intervening beyond political cleavages. In large international organizations, it is the hour of mobilization. The problematic of humanitarian intervention was implemented by Bernard Kouchner (see Bettati and Kouchner 1987). His efforts were fruitful, so much so that the United Nations resolution on the "free access to victims of catastrophes" (Resolution 43/131, December 8, 1988) substantially transformed the concept of the duty of intervention, substituting the *right of intervention*. As Kofi Annan, secretary-general of the UN, declared when he received the Nobel Peace Prize in 2001: "State sovereignty can no longer be used as a screen to mask systematic violations of human rights." The humanitarian obligation went from being marginal to taking on such a central role that it is even able to justify intervention in domains that normally fall under state competency.

In the logic of "without-borderism," the principle of nonintervention must stop covering the abuse of certain states in regard to human rights. The humanitarian sector is in charge of our most invaluable good: life. As a carrier of the ethics of solicitude, called on to intervene in a crisis situation, in a temporality different from that of routine politics, it transcends by definition all state reason. Suffering, destitution, prostrated bodies, and the imploring eyes of the children of the Third World: with all this distress, the traditional politics no longer seems able to square up. NGOs will thus be made—in partnership with the great international organizations—the promoters of a new world order connected to an ethic which authorizes them to circumvent and, if necessary, to subvert the constraints of national sovereignties and the small calculations of international diplomacy.

The invocation of human rights is the occasion of the mise-en-scène of evils that ravage the planet, whether they are due to the injustice of men or to the failures of the environment. "Humanitarian disasters"—an expression that can apply just as well to a natural disaster like a tsunami as to a genocide knowingly perpetrated against a population—are the occasion to mobilize the well-to-do with the support of images, speeches, and even media ceremonies. Since the "concert of the century" organized by Bob Geldof to help the victims of the Ethiopian famine up to the recent performances of Sting, we saw how, with the media's assistance, festive events intended for a worldwide public were built. They aim to diffuse a message that governments—and more generally everything in the realm of political representation—cannot, because they are stuck in the mud pit of power relations. This message is characterized by its universality; it is a message of resistance to the malefic forces threatening humans as well as an exaltation of life in all its forms, a message of peace and nonviolence. Carried by charismatic figures coming from the world of entertainment, this discourse is inseparable from the charitable gesture that it promotes.

We can wonder, along with Marcel Gauchet, if the influence of "human-rightism" is not the expression of a major crisis of political ideologies, on the one hand, and of the intensification of individualism, on the other. In a context marked by the vacancy of canonical references to tradition, progress, and even revolution, human rights comes to fill the vacuum and "represent the wide-open future" (Gauchet 2002, 349). This critical interpretation of the new shape of political correctness reveals, in the fog of a discourse clouded by ethics, one of the surest reasons of its success in the Western world. But the humanitarian sector does not only help in ideas; it also deploys a practical effectiveness on grounds where politics has not been effective. To come back to the "charity business" and these great worldwide demonstrations, it is impossible to ignore that they fall under a more general project of redistribution, on a philanthropic horizon whose purely material dimension is often underestimated. It is not only a question of promoting a policy, but also an *economy* of survival whose principles are not reducible to those that govern a policy of convivance. We would be wrong to think of the humanitarian sector as simply the negative of convivance, which comes, for want of anything better, to relay a democratic mechanism that is losing speed. We should wonder, rather, whether the humanitarian does not belong to another matrix by articulating ethics, economy, and citizenship in a paradigm that did not arise from a classical tradition of the social contract. That would explain, in part, why the speeches of politicians, still locked to the ideal of an *organization* (better, more just, etc.) of society, seem meager when confronted with the requirements of reality.

Let us now take a closer look. At the end of the 1980s, at the moment when "human-rightism" intrudes onto the world scene, this ideology appears as a criticism of the capacity and legitimacy of the state to answer a multitude of problems. The reiterated failures of postcolonial political structures to deal with the situations of shortages and endemic conflicts are combined with the cynicism expressed by their "developed" partners. At the end of the Cold War years, while the dynamic of neoliberal globalization intensifies, this discordance takes on a local and regional dimension seldom reached, making traditional protagonists seem overwhelmed and out of date. The state, but also political parties and trade unions, are confounded by modes of thinking and acting that are deployed in the simultaneity of the local and the global.

"Act local, think global": this maxim summarizes the humanitarian turn of the 1980s. A new space opens, with contours no longer limited to national borders. The NGO phenomenon takes on its full impact in this situation; without really understanding what it referred to, we note the expression of the "world civil society," affirming itself vis-à-vis the flippancy of politicians on subjects they can no longer control. In fact, the organizations structured on an international scale, able to mobilize within this framework, will see their role expanded. They simultaneously acquire a material base and a power of communication that enables them to become the lawyers of worldwide causes. The biggest NGOs—Care, Oxfam, Doctors without Borders, the World Wildlife Fund (WWF)—thus become the essential speakers in this new context. They intervene in a double register: through lobbyism and through large media campaigns. Moreover, large NGOs with humanitarian vocations widen their competencies to the field of development. With the multiplication of organizations arises the question of competition between NGOs in the humanitarian domain; hence the need for redeployment in order to position themselves as well as possible among the competition. More generally, the most recent period is marked by a complexification of the NGO phenomenon, which finds its echo in the increasingly frequent invocation of "civil society."

In the context of globalization, one notes a growing awareness of the impact of a type of actor who hitherto was almost completely eclipsed by the traditional protagonists of international politics. The fact that other voices can be expressed on the global scale and that immense campaigns can mobilize in the four corners of the world causes both hope and impatience among all those who became disillusioned with the partisan political mechanisms that dominated the twentieth century, and the ideologies that they conveyed. The collapse of the Communist bloc marks the end of a cycle and induces the increasingly widespread idea that the future will be built differently, according to a new exigency confronted with a globalization imposed by dominant economic interests. The hour is no longer about without-borderism; from now on the voice of alter-globalization makes itself heard with a strong power of seduction and mobilization. International civil society, whether or not it was born in Rio in 1992 or 1998 during the preparation for the convention prohibiting antipersonnel mines, undoubtedly appeared in its current representation for the first time in Seattle in 1999, and then in Porto Alegre, Montreal, Genoa, and so on.

NGOS are thus spontaneously identified with the representative actors of a world citizenry in construction. Some stages mark this evolution; initially, the repercussions of the

< >UN's Economic and Social Council resolution of 1996 were such that NGOs grew in stature and power as social partners alongside states and international institutions in the creation of international laws (Willetts 2000). By recognizing their moral authority, a quantifiable influence on processes of political decision making, one measures the emerging power of NGOS. At the same time, their competence and expertise in the (re)formulation of major international problems is legitimated, in domains such as human rights, the respect of biodiversity, the consideration of the greenhouse effect, and the creation of environmental standards (Arts 2003/4). A study of the newspaper *Le Monde* in December 2000 carried out in five continental countries reveals that 50 percent of the people questioned consider NGOS representative of the values they believe in, and only 11 percent say the same about governments. In France, NGOS appear three times more credible than governments, five times more than companies, and nine times more than the press. Asked about the reasons for the success of NGOS, the people questioned highlight their aggressiveness, their direct link with the public, their capacity to be united, the clearness of their ideals, and their aptitude to mobilize the media for positive use.

< >154

The entrance of NGOS as protagonists in transnational public space also caused many interrogations and criticisms. It is true that we have observed their rise to power since 1945, the date on which article 71 of the Charter of the United Nations allowed their participation in an advisory capacity in the UN's activities. It provides that the "Economic and Social Council (ECOSOC) can take all useful provisions to consult the nongovernmental organizations that deal with questions coming under their competence." It is in this article that the expression "nongovernmental organizations" appears for the first time. Before that, one spoke of "international associations." NGOs collaborated in drafting article 71, which does nothing but make official one type of practice already in force of the time of the Society of Nations (SDN). It should be noted, however, that NGO activity in international arenas remains limited and that during a score of years, between 1950 and 1971, observers were wary of NGOs' capacity for harm, especially on the international stage, more so than they were likely to acknowledge the organizations' positive contribution of expertise, even though that expertise was recognized.

During this period, NGOs took a new step toward recognition by being granted a consultant status to the ECOSOC in 1968. The organizations, however, had to apply for accreditation in order to obtain this status. The competition for accreditation is hard, and it causes discrimination between accredited and nonaccredited NGOs, the former depending on the UN's discretionary power to assign or withdraw the status. In 1992, at the time of the Conference of Rio, and spurred on by Kofi Annan, the UN acted in favor of facilitating the means for obtaining international accreditation by creating two distinct statuses: one as a consultant, the other as an observer. NGOs have experienced exponential growth for thirty years. In 1970 the ECOSOC had accredited 500 NGOs; today more than 2000 have accreditation. On the whole, there are approximately 38,000 in the world.

The presence of NGOs in fields hitherto directed by states

and representative, political, and trade union organizations has not gone without irritation and criticism. What annoys the diplomats and the politicians about the NGO phenomenon? By answering this question, we give ourselves the means of understanding what has shifted on the international scene with the arrival of these intruders. To take one example among others: at the UN-sponsored conference held in Rome in 1998 concerning the establishment of the International Criminal Court, NGOs were true partners in the negotiations. One could point out that the members of parliament of the concerned countries had been less informed about and involved in this process than the NGOs, "as if a dialogue, a competition and sometimes a partnership between [state] administration and NGO replaced the regular dialogue between government and parliament" (Sur 1999, 36).

Concerning the question of the role that NGOs now hope to play as a participant in the decisions taken at the transnational level, it is interesting to refer to how the European Commission responded to their insistence that they take part in the framework of a true institutional partnership. The Convention 124 drawn up by the Council of Europe did not satisfy NGOs who asked the European Commission to recognize their official consultant status based on the UN model. The commission rejected this system of accreditation of NGOs while affirming that, contrary to the system of international organizations, the decision-making process in the EU is above all else legitimated by the elected representatives of European people. One finds this argument developed in a report on the reinforcement of the partnership with NGOs, cosigned in 2000 by the president of the European Commission, Romano Prodi and Neil Kinnock, the U.K.'s commissioner on the European Commission.

At the root of the controversies concerning NGOS, one always finds an adjacent interrogation concerning the legitimacy of this type of organization, including skepticism with regard to their ambition of opening a new political space. It is true that NGOS tend to want to intervene on the international scene in fields (humanitarian, developmental, environmental) where the questions can no longer be settled on a state scale. At the same time, it is precisely a political space where transnational organizations—to start with, the UN—look, on their side, to impose themselves in the context of state supervision. They find in their partnership with NGOS the possibility of opening up the political playing field. NGOS are thus reinforced. As a result, the traditional democratic authorities, elected and governing, find competition on grounds where they are less at ease than in the routine of traditional political and trade union relations. We can understand the displeasing remarks made by former French foreign minister Hubert Védrine about NGOS, suspects of hubris, in their perseverance to encroach on the field of diplomacy. More generally, it is known that the French ministry of foreign affairs tolerates criticism poorly, especially when NGOS contest some of France's strategic choices.

Moreover, behind the reassuring facade of just causes and ethical voluntarism, do NGOS have a tendency to dissimulate their own flaws and even their own failures? The absence of true democratic control over their actions could be the source of their flawed way of functioning, also related to the competition that exists between NGOs in fields where the multiplication of supply is not always proportional to the limits of demand. For some critics, the implicit hierarchy and the competitiveness of NGOs toward financial backers can only exacerbate the tensions between old and new NGOs in the race to accreditation. In this context, the clearest consequence would be the renewal of a cleavage between North and South, in particular with regard to internet access, as a source of mobilization, as well as to access to expertise. Within the framework of their partnerships with local NGOs, those of the North tend to require the local organizations to provide the maximum of tangible evidence for their use of funds, implying a sometimes meddlesome control. Certain NGOs of the South have even preferred to return the money to donors than to be subjected to their requirements, often considered abusive. To rectify this situation, they try to increase their capacities of self-financing, but it is clear that the gap separating NGOs in the North and in the South remains quite wide.

The most complex question, continually addressed to NGOs, refers to their legitimacy. Are they, in the final analysis, the instrument of a self-proclaimed elite, a "militant jet set"? When we raise the problem of NGOs' *representativeness*, we are forced to acknowledge that their decisions are made by individuals who have not been elected. During international negotiations, they deal with government representatives who come from democratic procedures. The NGO leaders themselves can only find their legitimacy in the universality and cogency of the cause that they defend. They are self-proclaimed spokespeople of "civil society," a term whose usage is often unclear, both in regard to what it covers and whether using "civil society" does not intentionally flatten a universe whose diversity is then reduced to a standardizing expression. Through a discourse unified behind consensual slogans (the fight against poverty, for the reduction of the greenhouse effect, and for fair trade) diffuses a noncritical definition of "the general interest" and "universal goods." In addition, they implicitly refer to the existence of a community that would be the fruit of globalization.

On their side, NGOs answer this criticism concerning their legitimacy by presenting several arguments. The first relates to their proximity to the ground. They are directly confronted with humanitarian crises and poverty. It is their work in the field that makes them the essential spokespeople of groups which, without them, would be abandoned to destitution or precariousness. Another argument relates to their detachment compared to the often political motivations controlling governmental action. They are not pledged to any established order. Still another argument is that NGOs have a true capacity for expertise. Their actions are haloed by technical legitimacy. But that implies a reinforcement of the power of experts by the counter-evaluations that they bring; we are witnessing a "privatization" of international regulation. Regarding the environment or finance, on the question of debt, for example, or of ethical trade, the standards are discussed between consultants and actors of the commercial private sector, without political arbitration.

Paradoxically, in these debates, we undoubtedly lose sight of the essential. *The influence of NGOs and the audience that they gather among citizens are attributable to the fact that through them, we hear the echo of an entire rejected humanity, those who seem abandoned on behalf of modernity.* One of the most profound effects of globalization, of the new conflicts that it produces, such as "peaceful" profit seeking on a global scale, is to reduce a mass of humans to the state of pure waste, to *wasted lives*, according to the striking expression of the sociologist Zygmunt Bauman (2004). These human beings have lost their attributes as citizens and are now no more than "bare lives,"[2] populations shunted between a clandestine existence and refugee camps. But all these people are truly there, they keep knocking on the doors of the universe of the rich only to be generally rejected with a violence of which we are aware. And the place that nongovernmental organizations occupy in public space depends foremost on the action that they carry out to ensure the survival of these rejected humans.

2. Giorgio Agamben (2000), in reference to the Aristotelian distinction, contrasts "bare life" (*zoé*) to political life (*bios*).

One can certainly dispute criticisms of NGOs that highlight their lack of democratic legitimacy, by stressing that the authorities who claim to be the most democratic (parliaments and governments) are shown to be quite slow in reacting to human rights violations in the world or to the serious attacks of the planet's ecological integrity. Without NGOs and their transnational activism, laxity could have prevailed. Moreover, we would have undoubtedly never seen far-reaching initiatives like the Conference of Rio, which put the question of sustainable development on the agenda. The end of the twentieth century will be remembered for the progressive rise to power of a broad movement that came to counterbalance the most harmful effects of globalization.

Similarly, it is clear that we will not reconsider the participation of NGOs in important international negotiations. What has been introduced is another way of considering the political, not only as the everyday management of the polis, but also as related to the need for treating world affairs in a perspective where we take seriously the survival of the planet and the importance for the poorest to be heard in the public domain. This public space has been widened beyond the limits that institutions once set for it, in part because the scope of those institutions has been exceeded by the reach of globalization, as much on the economic level as on the ecological one. Even if we were wrong to undervalue "the resistance of the states" that Samy Cohen (2003) acknowledges and the way that intergovernmental relations continue to direct global destinies, there is no doubt that NGOs introduced a new situation, thanks to their privileged partnership with large transnational organizations. We are seeing the advent of forms of action privileging lobbyism and media pressure at the cost of traditional practices of diplomacy centered on respecting certain balances, including the old argument of power relations in the background. However, if this kind of situation functions within a framework that puts a premium on the reference to the nation, when NGOs claim the *causes* they defend by ignoring arguments about national borders, then there is a risk of disorder in the well-oiled play of state powers and international organizations. From one day to the next, complicity can be endangered by the revelation of the unacceptable. In this way, even with a subaltern appearance in terms of their political role, these transnational actors have gained an impact of sufficient strength that states must anticipate the effects of what NGOs do when developing state strategies. We would be wrong, however, to lock ourselves in a debate of an altogether academic nature, when it is now a more profound question of opening our representations and our apprehension of the political to interrogations that hitherto eluded them.

From this point of view, it seems to me that the grand question projected by NGOS in the center of public space is that of the economy of survival, so that they force nolens volens the traditional sphere of international relations to take on a new form of reflexivity centered on this economy. To give one example of this process, I will take the case of the campaigns carried out by the Oxfam organization. The Oxford Committee for Famine Relief was created in 1942 by two academics and a British businessman to provide food to Greece, which was then occupied by the Nazis and suffering from the Allied blockade. They put together 12,000 pounds that they gave to the Greek Red Cross. After the war, the organization intervened in India to overcome a famine in Bihar. Thereafter, it was present in all the campaigns against hunger and misery in the countries of the South, from battered Cambodia in 1979 to devastated Ethiopia to the refugee camps of Rwanda in 1994.

More recently, from Kosovo to Mozambique, from Sudan to Bangladesh, there is no humanitarian emergency that Oxfam misses. It also intervenes in the West in impoverished zones. Oxfam has become one of the most prominent NGOS in the humanitarian field. On its website, it summarizes its principles of action in the following way: "We work with the poor," "We influence the powerful," "We give everyone a hand." These are ways of saying that it combines three essential activities: on one side, development and humanitarian aid; on another, campaigns and lobbying to influence international policies and practices; finally, the mobilization of the general public concerning these issues.

With an annual budget of $1.3 billion, Oxfam has the means for its multiple ambitions. Today, it is a confederation of twelve organizations, operating in several countries of Europe, Canada, the United States, Australia, Hong Kong, and Africa, as well as a network of active associations in more than one hundred countries. Oxfam counts 200,000 members and employs 3,500 permanent workers; in addition to its various organizations, it opened offices in London, Brussels, Geneva, and New York, where the British Parliament, the European Commission, the WTO, and the UN sit, respectively. I went to Broad Street, in the center of Oxford, where the head office of Oxfam Great Britain and international Oxfam occupies two entire buildings. In one of them are gathered, on several floors, the personnel who devote themselves to campaign organization and media relationships. On the other side of the street, an "Oxfam shop" sells inexpensive products, which are in fact gifts from British people. The collected money makes it possible to promote actions on the ground. If Max Havelaar was a pioneer by opening the first fair trade store in the Netherlands at the end of the 1960s, Oxfam is now at the head of the movement, with 850 shops open in Great Britain.

Oxfam's work in the development and humanitarian aid sectors falls under a vaster strategy that begins with the principle that "poverty is a state of impotence in which people are not able to exercise their rights." These rights are five: the right to a sustainable means of subsistence, the right to basic social services, the right to life and safety, the right to be heard, and the right to an identity. The defense of economic and social rights constitutes the foundation of the multi-annual strategic plans that Oxfam implements. Beginning in the 1960s, Oxfam launched what was going to become the great adventure of free trade by creating bonds with producers in developing countries and finding outlets for their products, as well as relentlessly recovering clothing and other secondhand goods that it resells at low prices.

"Towards World Equity"—that was the title of Oxfam's Strategic Plan 2001–2004. It especially aimed at the improvement of southern countries' access to the market. "For every 100 euros generated by the world trade, 3 go to developing countries." On the basis of this observation, Oxfam decided to conduct a campaign for a fairer globalization. In this objective, it invested in the preparation of the new cycle of negotiations that were to open the WTO meeting in Cancun in September 2003. Oxfam preached the redeployment of agricultural subsidies toward social and environmental objectives and the defense of poor countries' rights to protect their agricultural markets. These preoccupations are also found in other organizations, such as Brothers of Men, in which, beginning in the 1980s, the fight against "bad development" provoked an increasingly profound partnership with autochthonous peoples.

Similarly, professional organizations like the Confédération Paysanne (Farmers Confederation) preach the adoption of common strategies with southern countries: one of the strong points from this perspective is the criticism of agricultural subsidies that support northern countries and handicap the economy of southern countries. Rather than sticking to a humanitarian message that, in fact, is not enough to remedy inequalities, it initiated a transnational reflection on the issue of poor countries' access to markets. These reflections were manifested in clearly argued studies — for example, about the sugar and textile industries, as well as in campaigns carried out jointly on the European scale.

As we can see, this type of NGO does not only intervene on the ground by multiplying field initiatives of development

and equitable trade. It implements a total strategy based on a general vision of the economy that contests the excesses of neoliberalism. Oxfam does not dispute the liberalization of exchanges in itself but rather the fact that this liberalization takes place without consideration of the specific situations of the poorest countries and by supporting the maintenance of agricultural subsidies for certain types of products both in Europe and in the United States, which caused real dumping in the agricultural sector.

"To put trade at the service of sustainable development . . . and not the opposite" was one of the slogans of the extremely effective campaign that Oxfam conducted on the margins of the interministerial conference in Cancun in 2003. At the beginning, the negotiations were engaged and the agreement on poor countries' access to drugs was adopted, but the tension increased when four countries — Benin, Burkina Faso, Chad, and Mali — gave a report on the importance that cotton production and trade has for their economies. Referencing the imbalance resulting from the subsidies in this sector to producers in rich countries, they asked for the suppression of these subsidies. This sectorial initiative on cotton crystallized the opposition of poor countries, led by India, Brazil, Kenya, and China, against the United States and Europe. In this part of the conflict, the NGOs, with Oxfam in the lead, took up the cause of developing countries. Even before the beginning of the conference, Oxfam had started a petition called "The Big Noise" denouncing the injustice of international trade rules. The petition collected three million signatures from around the world. It was grandly given to the director general of the WTO by Chris Martin, lead singer of the British group Coldplay, and Adrian Lovett, director of Oxfam campaigns and communication. The group, accompanied by a multitude of journalists, had just returned from a visit with Mexican corn producers during which they had been able to see the difficult living and working conditions of these farmers. Parallel media events (concerts, CDs of the Big Noise) and one week of action at the European Parliament echoed by official statements and analyses diffused on the website of the organization helped increase the pressure.

During the few days of the meeting in Cancun, the Oxfam spokespeople were not satisfied with leading demonstrations; they also played the part of counselor for the poor countries and popularized their position with the media by holding several press conferences. The NGO had thus transformed the conference into a "morality play," as a member of the EU delegation described it, not without bitterness. It is interesting to note that a dialogue within the framework of a focus group had been established between the European commissioner in charge of foreign trade and the NGOs, in which the NGOs were informed and consulted. The competence of an organization like Oxfam on agro-alimentary subjects is indeed recognized: it has its own experts, including high-level economists, whom the European Commission consulted concerning delicate issues such as the sugar trade, in which the pressure of lobbies is particularly strong. In Cancun, the EU delegation included NGO representatives who, because of their independence and convictions about fair trade, defended positions diametrically opposed to those of the rest of the delegation.

Reporting the events, some accused Oxfam of playing a "double game"; on the one hand, that of seriousness and expertise, and, on the other, that of systematic contestation, even if it meant spoiling the negotiation. In any case the final failure of the conference clarified the impact of this type of organization as the carrier of a project that it imposes in the face of the diplomatic play of nation-states. Not that they enter directly into this play: in Cancun, NGOs were not present in the room where the inter-ministerial conference took place. Their force rests in the way they transform what is only a brief exercise in interstate relations into a true event, in their capacity to produce a spectacle of the immemorial confrontation between good and evil. One of the documents diffused by the Oxfam website on the failure of the meeting is significantly entitled "The Good, The Bad, and the Dubious" (or, in translation, poor countries, the United States, and Europe). The high number of Oxfam spokespeople among official negotiators is often mocked, whereas certain countries do not even have the means of paying the traveling expenses of their representatives.

In its own way, this globalized organization with remarkable logistics constitutes a power that it is now necessary to reckon with. If we try to analyze the nature of this power, we can see the combination of several elements: an economic base, professionalism, entrepreneurial initiative, media impact, and, last but not least, the prevalence of the themes of survival in their action and discourse. These features are not specific to Oxfam; we find them in other large NGOs. In addition to contributions and gifts, the great humanitarian organizations receive the support of important national and international institutions. The World Bank gave Oxfam-Quebec $1 million to conclude a project of reintegration of street children in the urban zones of the Democratic Republic of Congo. "NGOs that ignore the role of the [World] Bank in the development of strategies of assistance on the global, national, and local levels, do so at their own risk," observed John Ruthrauff, the principal counselor of Oxfam America.

The amount of international subsidies and national public financing that NGOs receive is surpassed by private funds, which represent the largest share of NGO financial support. Organizations such as the World Wildlife Fund (WWF) developed collaborations with companies from the licensing of products to a conservation partnership. Similarly, Max Havelaar, the pioneering NGO of fair trade, delivered its label to tea and coffee brands, marking a respect for certain ethical principles. Its label is connected to nearly a quarter of the coffee sector's 20 million workers worldwide; the NGO receives about 13 cents per kilo of coffee beans that they label "fair trade."

NGOS are continually looking for new modes of financing to enable them to develop their activities. This situation constrains them to privilege, in the humanitarian field, the techniques of marketing. Like private companies, NGOS compete among themselves, which encourages them to seek good "positionings" (and why not "good" victims?) to provoke donors' favors. They devote more and more money to communication and fundraising, and do not hesitate to implement an administration anxious to fulfill their financers' requirements of social profitability. In certain sectors, the high growth of institutional financing has perverse effects because it leads to support in the zones where the emergencies have the most media coverage, at the expense of other less media-friendly areas.

Sylvie Brunel, who directed Action against Hunger, stresses that while the budget of this organization multiplied by ten between 1989 and 2001, private givers, who went from 80,000 to 450,000, account for no more than 23 percent of the budget in 2000 against 50 percent in 1989. This preeminence of official backers results in a new kind of framing, with NGOS progressively becoming "subcontractors of public power." We observe, on the other hand, a restriction of the space of intervention of these organizations, which supports the development of geographical areas in which the state donors, or the agencies that they finance, submit NGO financing to framework agreements (*Cahiers Français* 2001). We understand that sometimes even those who work for NGOS come to question the conditions that their organizations are working under, because of their dependence on both public and private financing to enable them to carry out their activities.

These criticisms reflect the fact that NGOs fall under a logic which is not the same as for public organizations, but rather brings them closer to the world of enterprise. At Oxfam, the managers whom I met came from the private realm where they had been executives. For example, the representative of the organization in Geneva began in a development bank in the United States; in Oxford one of the executives used to manage British Petroleum in Zambia. One also finds former EU civil servants. The fact that the personnel of NGOs come from the elite of companies or large international organizations explains why the militancy of their origins made way for the realism of management methods.

This professionalization, in particular regarding the search for funds, imposes a style of communication that influences the NGO discourse and makes it conform to the mode of expression prevailing in the commercial world. It is quite obvious that, to go past the stage of denunciation and to avoid being locked into a mission of emergency therapy, NGOs are confronted with the need to institutionalize themselves in their relation to public financing. They find themselves metamorphosed, which weighs on their autonomy and can modify their associative culture. Aren't we now dealing with a new pecking order or rather with a new group whose function would be that of the beggars' interpreter among the powerful? It is also true that NGOs are the carriers of a new rationality that takes its place beside the logic of bureaucracy profits (see Massiah 2000); we would thus see the emergence of a new logic of territorialization and mutualization which complicates the traditional relations between political power and economic power, between trade unions and companies.

In an analysis devoted to the evolution of the contemporary international system, T. Biersteker and R. Hall (2001) signal the rise in power of private authority and the propensity of states to give this private authority an increasingly important place. According to these authors, there are three types of private authority: market power, moral authority, and illicit power. NGOs exert a moral authority; they fall under private international regimes. The international regimes are characterized as processes of decision making and definition of the problems that need to be solved. There is an international regime dedicated to stopping the proliferation of weapons of mass destruction, just as there are some that deal with pollution in certain areas of the world. These regimes are the fruit of intergovernmental negotiations and are equipped with power, institutionalized by the governments. The private international regimes prepare decisions and fix the agendas in the domain of the transnational regulation of environmental questions. "They contribute to the creation of global civil society, in which important transnational decisions are made in a private way" (Biersteker and Hall 2001, 17). For Biersteker and Hall, NGO authority is based foremost on their capacity to propose the list of topics to be negotiated. It is the result of a true lobbyism that requires a very intense presence in the international arena. Their authority also comes from their capacity of expertise. Lastly, it is necessary to insist on the moral character of NGO authority, which stems from their positioning in social fields and their demonstrated progressivism.

We can add that one of the objective functions of NGOS consists in managing the junction between the center and the peripheries, and especially in reinforcing the pressure of the peripheries on the center. From the point of view of NGOS, it is important to influence international powers by putting the problem of disorders created by globalization in the foreground, whether social and human abuses, ecological disorders, or the deepening of the gap between the North and the South. One of the results the NGOS can take pride in is to have imposed the responsibility principle on the international scene, by making it the moral obligation of states to either act or repair. Their many campaigns caused governmental actors to become aware that the survival of humanity passes through the interdependence of the units that make it up and that there is a strong solidarity between generations. As Bertrand Badie (1999) suggests, the responsibility principle would tend to overtake the traditional principle of sovereignty that put its stamp on international relations until the last quarter of the twentieth century.

Should we be surprised that the qualitative change that NGOS experienced caused an ensemble of interrogations that reflect the critical stances that I mentioned? The tensions that surfaced initially concerned the modes of managing civil society: is it necessary to make the functioning of NGOS evolve in the direction of rationalization, in conformity with the model of the most powerful private companies? Or must they embody above all the ideal of activism and solidarity in line with the associative movement in which they have their roots?

These questions do nothing but reflect the orientation that is constitutive of NGOS. They are part of a very different tradition from that which characterized the triumph of the welfare state in a country like France. In the Anglo-Saxon world, the importance of voluntary help and private charitable initiatives is related to the role that the actors of civil society take in the provision of social services, regarded as part of the exclusive terrain of the state in France. North Americans invented the expression "nonprofit sector" to distinguish this field from business and government. They also designate it as the "third sector." The installation of the third sector, with its fabric of associations subsidized by foundations and with its rise to power after World War II, resulted in the creation of an original model in which private initiatives play an essential part; the third sector wants to be independent. The multiplicity of financings, via charitable gifts, foundations, and governmental assistance, is supposed to allow the preservation of this autonomy. Similarly, pluralism and the absence of centralization are regarded as essential conditions to effectively ensure the development of the "third sector." This step is very different from the French concept of social solidarity: it aims at putting private investments at the service of the collective interest.

It has nothing in common with the French *service public*, whose subsidies and governance mainly involve public authorities in a context where the general will is embodied by the state, it alone carrying a legitimacy recognized by all citizens. In France, public resources provide nearly 60 percent of the financial support of the nonprofit sector, whereas they account for only 30 percent in the United States. Of course, the third sector in the United States, which accounts for 6.9 percent of total employment today, did not develop in the margins of the state, and the great social programs were carried out within the framework of collaboration between private organizations, such as the Ford Foundation, and the federal government. It appears very natural in this context that an industry tycoon deals with actions targeting the development of science or environmental protection. During an earlier study, some philanthropists I met were none other than the heads of businesses who had become billionaires and were devoting a portion of their money and their energy to the nonprofit sector. In Seattle, Paul Brainerd, the inventor of PageMaker software, created a foundation with $15 million in resources, and $2 million are allotted each year to associations. The objective is to promote the preservation of the environment along the northwest coast, affected in certain areas by rapid population increase.

Like Carnegie and Rockefeller, who had worked in the field of education and health, Brainerd practices "scientific charity" in his own way. But unlike earlier patrons, the "new philanthropists" are concerned with the yield of their initiatives. According to them, there is no reason *not* to apply the methods that proved their effectiveness within the framework of the most modern capitalism. The concept of a social business elaborated by the ideologists of the new economy aims at overcoming the cleavage between the for-profit sphere and the nonprofit sphere and at legitimating the use of venture capital techniques in a domain where hitherto the concept of profitability made no sense whatsoever.

To improve the non-lucrative sector, it is also necessary to know how to take risks. The foundations must maintain the same kinds of relations with the organizations they finance as venture capitalists maintain with the start-ups they support. From this necessity came the idea to promote venture philanthropy, which caused a debate within the third sector on financing strategies and their effective impact. In this conception, the question of investment yield becomes central: it is important to measure the performances of associations and to quantify the results obtained in a field hitherto reticent about using this kind of evaluation. The spirit that animates modern capitalism now penetrates the domains that had long been closed to it.

It is thus not without interest to refer to the debate ruffling the philanthropy milieu in the United States, which opposes the traditional advocates of volunteering to the sycophants of "venture philanthropy" (see Abélès 2002; Guilhot 2004), in order to understand the discussions relating to the entrepreneurial vocation of NGOs. From this point of view, NGOs should become more professional and yield to the principles that prevail in the commercial universe; hence the need for taking "return on investment" into account and for obtaining personnel recruited more on criteria of competence and effectiveness with regard to moral engagement. The danger that the adversaries of this change denounce lies in the seizure of power by a lobbying and public relations elite, increasingly cut off from social and human problems that are at the root of NGO activity.

We can just as well wonder whether the specificity of NGOs is not due precisely to a double anchoring: political in terms of actors in the global polis, and economic in terms of companies centered on survival. From the political point of view, NGOs can pride themselves on bringing "the voice of those without voices" to the public sphere, in making suffering heard, this "misery of the world" present in the most removed corners of the planet. These organizations would be the vectors of policy—through their actions and how they dramatize the misery of a world subject to multiple forms of exploitation and inequalities—insofar as they show what is hidden in the process of neoliberal globalization and make a discordant discourse heard, faced with the well-articulated statements of the dominant forces. To borrow the definition suggested by Jacques Rancière, we are certainly dealing with politics. It is a mode of demonstration that subverts the *partage du sensible* (the distribution of the sensible)—the configuration which defines the sharing and the shares—by reintroducing those whom Rancière calls *"les sans-part"* (people without shares) (Rancière 2002, 53). The failure of Cancun is, in this way, exemplary. A little like the plebeians who withdraw from Aventin, causing the Roman patricians to suddenly realize that the plebeians are humans like themselves, and thus equal, the attitude of the G21 countries refusing to sign the agreement brought by the patricians of globalization puts this share of those without shares (*le part des sans-part*) into the middle of the negotiation, something which the regulated play of diplomacy tends to make invisible.

When the actions of NGOs are considered, it is undeniable that they contribute to the creation of breaking points that allow the introduction of a political space where the voice of those without voices can be heard. In this way, even if we can legitimately challenge their claims to embody "civil society," what is certain is that they induce disorder and discordance in the interstate concert. Is this to say that these organizations are in themselves subversive or of a different nature than other international institutions? By observing the professionalism of NGOs, their executives' membership in the club of globalized elites, we quickly understand that these leaders have nothing in common with the ideal of the professional revolutionist who directed the cosmopolitan militancy of the past. In reality, what motivates managers in charge of the big NGOs to work in the nonprofit arena instead of in the private sector or in the great international institutions is generally an engagement of the ethical type. This ethical engagement does not imply calling the capitalist system into question and introducing a new social order.

As I observed among Californian entrepreneurs, the invocation of ethical values does not concern spiritual enrichment, but proves to be completely coherent with an economic project centered on personal freedom articulated harmoniously with the collectivity. He who wrote, "We let ourselves believe that in an equitable environment, individuals and communities can become the best they can be," is not a great reformer but, instead, one of the most skilled businessmen of his generation: Pierre Omidyar, the creator of eBay. The fact that there are large firms that now claim to practice "virtuous capitalism" and intend to make ethical standards prevail does nothing but reinforce a more general movement in which "multinationals of civic virtue" take part (see Dezalay and Garth 1996). Political effects that NGOs produce are mainly due to their multisite position — both in the high ranks of the international arena as well as in peripheral areas — and to the back-and-forth that they establish between the voices of the periphery and the secret meetings of the center.

We should never forget, however, that large humanitarian and development organizations, who are *private actors*, maintain, with their status and their operating mode, a strong complicity with the business universe. Like businesses, NGOs arose foremost from the economic sphere. As soon as we point toward their political dimension because of the effects they produce in the public realm, it is important to add that their impact is related to the primordially economic character of their action. We place ourselves in the field of the economy of survival that constitutes the specific field of intervention of these organizations. One spontaneously associates the exchange of the goods and the prevalence of the market to the economy. Opening of markets, increasingly intense circulation of goods — this is how the reality of globalized exchange presents itself. In this context, the economy of survival seems to contradict the principles governing the market economy. Whereas the latter exalts the freedom of exchange, the former underlines the need for human intervention. Moreover, the object of the economy of survival—above all, bare life, the excluded, the needy, and the humanitarian emergency—concerns actions antithetic to economic principles.

The gift without counterpart—and not exchange—is the principle of humanitarian action. Marcel Mauss wrote that the gift is "one of the human foundations on which our societies are built" (Mauss 1990 [1950], 4). Admittedly, the practices he analyses are those of traditional societies in Melanesia, Polynesia, Alaska, and northwestern America. The *kula* of the Trobrianders or the potlatch of the Tlingit and the Haïda are quite far from contemporary philanthropic initiatives. Mauss, however, did not hesitate to generalize his insight, even extrapolating "moral conclusions" in which he evokes the "uses" of his time, the role of social security systems and mutual benefit societies instituted within the framework of trade unions and professional associations, as well as the coverage of social security by certain states. Being prescriptive, he recommends an effort by wealthy classes to contribute to the collective wellbeing: "As is happening in English-speaking countries and so many other contemporary societies, whether made up of savages or the highly civilized, the rich must come back to considering themselves—freely and also by obligation—as the financial guardians of their fellow-citizens" (1990 [1950], 68–69).

By stressing the responsibility of rich people, the author of *The Gift* illustrates the need for developing practices based on solidarity in counterpoint to the market economy. Can one, however, speak about a *complementarity* between the market economy and the economy of survival? Can the economy of survival seem a possible alternative to the market and the increasing dehumanization of commercial relations? If Mauss also largely inspires the most radical partisans of an alter-economy or an economy based on solidarity, it is less because they refer to the paradigm of the gift and reciprocity and more that they see in the exemption from payment, and especially in the claim of universal citizenship, the horizon of a promising utopia. By leaning on the experience of intermediate institutions that structure the experiments of an economy based on solidarity, they seek to promote forms of action that combine institutional initiatives inside the economic world, like the funds of ethical investments, the label "fair trade," or the projects of citizen enterprise. Thus, drawing on Mauss and Karl Polanyi, the solidarity economy uses models other than those of self-regulation. It wants to institute a true hybridization between the monetary bond and the social bond. The ambition of a "plural economy" appears on the horizon, where the economy of public goods, the economy of reciprocity, interdependent and associative, and the cash economy would coexist, intertwined with one another.

What gives the NGO phenomenon its rather unusual character is that the activity of these organizations is focused on the economy of survival. Consequently, their urgency-imbued stance also fits with an outlook of a future made uncertain by threats engendered by the merchandization of the universe. The economy of survival carries within it the issue of sustainability. We see this clearly in the area of the environment, where catastrophes regularly give us cause to evoke the responsibility of a productivist development model centered on profit. The reactions of the populations of developed countries to the great recent natural disasters are entirely symptomatic of the response elicited by crisis situations. We saw this at the time of the Asian Tsunami—the tidal wave that, in December 2003, ravaged the coasts of a dozen South Asian countries, leaving in its wake hundreds of thousands dead. We witnessed at this time an immense outpouring of collective generosity. The intensity of the solidarity can be explained by the timing (the announcement of the catastrophe in the middle of the holiday period, and the feeling of living in peace and prosperity at a moment when others were abruptly stricken) and by the fact that westerners had been more directly affected than had been the case during other catastrophes (holidaymakers on the Asian coasts had not been spared).

Other than the afflux of public finances, very large gifts came from the private sector. To cite only the big pharmaceutical companies: Pfizer gave $10 million to charitable organizations operating in the region as well as $25 million worth of medicine; Abbott Laboratories distributed $4 million, half in cash and half in medicine and food; Bristol-Myers Squibb gave $1 million; Johnson & Johnson gave $2 million. The number-one finance company in the world, Citigroup, distributed $3 million, between the Red Cross, local NGOS, and on-site reconstruction. $2 million came from Wal-Mart, which collected money in its stores.

Following the tsunami, the mobilized NGOS appealed to private individuals, and here we see the impact of the economy of survival on individual behavior. The sheer scale of private donations shows it, particularly in Europe and the United States. Even in a country like France, not usually noted for great charitable enthusiasm,[1] individual rallying to the cause took an impressive turn, in the shape of a veritable "humanitarian Telethon." In one day, text-message donations reached over €1 million. Looking back, what is striking about the breakdown of the donations is the fact that the amount of private donations almost reached that of the effort agreed to by the state. This was an unprecedented phenomenon, suggesting that the citizens wanted to express their commitment to the humanitarian effort directly. In this context, the use of technologies like the internet or text messaging—which make it possible to be directly involved in a global-level action while being confined to a local site—contributes to changing the traditional order of things. The individual can now step to the fore as a global player.

In the face of the traditional mediations embodied by national governments, a global donor action group is forming. This is embodied in the media in two ways: On the one side, we are shown people admirably involving themselves in order to come to the aid of victims, either on the ground or by inciting mobilization in their community or company. These people, "like you and me," acquire the status of the representative of the charitable collective. On the other side, a differ-

1. According to the *Observatoire de la Générosité et du Mécénat*, only 46 percent of the French population are regular donors, compared to 75 percent of Americans.

ent type of representation of the charitable élan is illustrated by emblematic figures of the humanitarian such as Mother Theresa or Abbé Pierre and Bernard Kouchner in France. And politicians show deference and humility toward these figures.

The remarkable aspect is the manner in which the political authority increasingly steps aside when confronted with types of action and discourse that deal with issues of global impact and have a relationship with our survival. Politicians take advantage of the cachet of these emblematic figures, or, when failing to do so, are content to manage the day-to-day crisis situations with which they are confronted. If by politics we mean the relationship that unites the individual with the group and the way in which the individual sees his integration into the city, we may well wonder if, on this level, there is not some profound change going on. In fact, our behaviors and the priorities that determine group action, plus the very fact that rallying of this nature and extent is possible when confronted with this type of catastrophe, reflect both anxiety and new awareness. The new awareness is that the world we live in may disappear and that, eventually, the survival of the species is threatened. This reaction is absolutely consistent with the response elicited by the theme of sustainability. Without doubt, it expresses an even more profound "anthropological anxiety." The NGO phenomenon fits into this perception, where tragic events regularly remind humans of the precarious nature of their situation.

In the case of the tsunami, the emotion triggered by the catastrophe had the paradoxical effect that one of the biggest

NGOS, Doctors without Borders, asked donors to stop giving, in the name of honesty and transparency. The NGO had already received €40 million. When other organizations criticized this decision, which could discourage future giving, and Action against Hunger accused Doctors without Borders of having "rich peoples' problems, whereas we deal with poor peoples' problems," Doctors without Borders invoked the demand of "traceability of payments received." In other words, the role of an NGO is not to accumulate amounts of money that it will then distribute when it feels like it among different humanitarian projects. It matters that donors know that their money is used for the cause that has mobilized them. The ethical concern that conditions this attitude is inseparable from a more general conception of management of the economy of survival. Here, we find the idea that the humanitarian association is accountable and that the amount of gifts alone does not guarantee their effectiveness. In parallel, the issue of "return on investment" is raised. Ethics and rationality come together to determine the application of the economy of solidarity.

Although these practices have different ends from those of the market economy, it is clear that forms of complementarity can exist between the economy of survival and globalized capitalism. Not only can the former function as a pressure valve for the latter, but, as we can see, the economy of survival is inspired by the modes of management that globalized capitalism developed. We could thus argue that—far from embodying an alternative project—humanitarian workers, the champions of fair trade, simply comfort the global system. A clear gap exists between the radical positions that confront this system head-on and the system and discourse of big NGOs, like Oxfam and the WWF, that are engaged in the fight against inequalities without questioning the market economy.

Projects of an ethical vocation, which aim at rebalancing commercial relations between producers and workers of the South and consumers of the North, hope to make certain fundamental principles prevail: the definition of a fair price allowing the producer and his family to live with dignity; working conditions corresponding at least to the standards of the International Labour Organization; criteria considered to mark "progress." They contest the reductive character of concepts that exalt the *homo economicus* and that make money and market into an end rather than a means. For them it is necessary to give the individual subject of the economy the sense of the values and relations which, in their complexity, give sense to life and express the dignity of the human condition. This exaltation of the individual is obvious in the conceptions that the ideologists of fair trade develop — beginning with the founder of Grameen Bank in Bangladesh, Muhammad Yunus, when he insists on the irreplaceable role of independent work.

Certainly, today, organizations whose purpose is the economy of survival represent a powerful opposition force. The NGOs and the social movements have clearly never fought as hard as they do now. They brought about the failure of the Multilateral Agreement on Investment (MAI) — proposed by the Organization for Economic Co-operation and Development (OECD) and largely favorable to entrepreneurism. They caused powerful genetic engineering companies in Europe to back off. We saw them play a leading role in the failure of the WTO negotiations in Cancun, where cotton producers in developing countries rejected an agreement that the United States wanted to impose on them. Gradually, political and economic powers have understood that they now really have to "reckon with" what is referred to under the controversial label of "civil society." On the NGO side, the question on the table is now whether to follow a strategy of automatic protest by favoring the tribunal function or to contribute to global governance by gaining acceptance for their views—which would involve the use of both pressure and negotiation. An organization like Oxfam, which played a leading role in the failure of the Cancun conference, still claims to support the existence of the WTO, inasmuch as the latter means the implementation of regulation on a global scale.

The aim of these NGOs is not to reject the market economy, but rather to establish a "connection" between the problems of people in the field and the global governance viewpoint and bring out the effects of this within that market economy. This is how to get concrete results and allow the southern countries to have access to worldwide trade, in giving them a chance to improve their economic situation. What is new in terms of the charitable purpose of the NGOs is not only their ability to connect the humanitarian problem to that of development but also the way in which they have been able to link the issue of development to that of global governance, on the basis of interpellations coming from poverty and concerning the distribution of wealth. It is not a matter of accepting the rules of the game as laid down by the WTO as an intangible fact, but of publicizing, in this framework, the main question, which can be summed up in the following way: why does the regulation of international trade tend to favor preferential systems that benefit the rich countries?

W e are, however, able to see the divide between movements that lambaste the WTO for representing neoliberal hegemony and NGOs who want to participate in the regulating process. The "connectionist" point of view was the target of a violent critique by Walden Bello, of the organization Focus on the Global South, who sees evidence of the acceptance of neoliberalism in the "connectionist" perspective. He disputes the position supporting market access to developing countries because, according to him, it is the absolute power of the market that must be radically reevaluated. There is a divide that separates pragmatic NGOs focused on reform and movements that contest the system as a whole. The embodiment of the latter, the Association for the Taxation of Financial Transactions for the Aid of Citizens (ATTAC), was created in the context of the mobilization against the Multilateral Agreement on Investment (MAI) following the publication of Ignacio Ramonet's editorial of December 1997 in *Le Monde Diplomatique*, significantly entitled "Disarming the Markets." The author decries financial capital, "which is putting people in a state of generalized insecurity." He targets the promoters of globalization, particularly the "IMF, World Bank, OECD, and WTO constellation," as "power without society" that leaves "societies without power."

The originality of ATTAC compared to social movements formed earlier lies in locating its struggles in the realm of globalization, by highlighting the impotence of states when faced with the financial markets that govern the planet. The denunciation of the MAI, which allowed the liberalization of multinational firms' investment conditions in states that signed the agreement, targeted the faceless power that ATTAC continues to challenge — without, however, presenting a clear alternative. Confronted with this power without society, it was unable to propose a political framework adequate to the evolution of present forces or the profound transformation of organizational forms. Thus, faced with the prospect of a change in scale — the idea of a Europeanization of power and political struggles — the tendency arises to fasten oneself to the nostalgic base of national sovereignty, and even to privilege strategies of proximity, the ultimate defense against the aggression of neoliberalism. It still remains — notwithstanding the orientation which, in the long term, will prevail — that these social dynamics have registered the thematic of inequalities within a globalized framework. This in turn amplifies the theme of threat: "generalized insecurity" takes on its full magnitude; it is the consequence of agitations impossible to control, of the mysterious "power without society."

Radical alter-globalizationists see themselves as making no concessions to the world system — which they intend to bring down. They opt for a "breaking-off" and champion this in the major international forums. This explains the fracture existing at the heart of this movement, of heterogeneous membership, regularly expressed at major events that bring together self-styled alter-globalizationists at a European and global level. It is noticeable, in fact, that the dividing lines are not always that sharply defined. To take the case of Oxfam, one of it components, Oxfam Solidarity (Jennar 2004), has taken a radical position from which Oxfam International has very clearly distanced itself.

The fact remains that even big NGOs that participate fully in the system of international relations simultaneously conduct violently anti-establishment campaigns. They have been accused of playing a double game, by simultaneously cultivating protest and negotiation. But isn't such duality an integral part of this kind of organization? And, above all, are we not seeing a mode of governance taking shape that will tend to integrate opponents into a broader dynamic? This is the argument of Ulrich Beck, according to whom the "cosmo-political era" we have entered is characterized by "a system of enemies without enemies" integrating governments and protestors. We are finally seeing them coming together on topics where they once seemed opposed on all points, such as the canceling of the debt of the poorest countries. Similarly, many leaders recognize the value of the Tobin tax. Despite his anchoring on the right, Jacques Chirac, facing the floor of business owners joined together in Davos, uses the same emphasis as third-world leaders when he contests "the blind economic forces [that] accentuate the marginalization of the weakest." As the correspondent of the French daily *Libéra-*

tion observed, "When they left the conference room, two vice presidents of Dupont, the American chemical company, did not hide their perplexity" (January 27, 2005).[1] Of this paradoxical fraternization, the most obvious example is George Soros, who is simultaneously an unscrupulous speculator and radical critic of the excesses of the market, a well-informed contractor and a remarkable philanthropist. Are NGOs therefore "the conscience of governments" (Beck 2003, 523)? Whatever the case, the links being forged between companies and nongovernmental organizations are evidence of this new order: Coca-Cola is helping the French humanitarian association Secours Populaire, the Carrefour supermarket chain is supporting the Fédération Internationale des Droits de l'Homme (the International Federation for Human Rights), Havas is contributing to the efforts of Care, and so on.

A more complex game is taking shape, where the partners of transnational institutions are no longer only states and international organizations that have emerged out of governmental wishes. Now, moral and economic "private authorities," NGOs and companies, have joined in. It is a game in which the weapon of collective rallying, heavily covered in the media, has an important place, but where the practice of partnerships and negotiating is very real. It is relevant to

1. The same writer added: "We sometimes end up promoting the social and environmental responsibility of both businesses and states. The future of globalization is not in an economy of social dumping or natural resource waste, but in the respect of social rights, in the general elevation of the quality of life, and in the respectful development of ecological equilibrium" (*Libération*, January 27, 2005).

note the way in which the one-on-one debate is unfolding around the virtually simultaneous "staging" of the Davos and Porto Alegre forums — the former bringing together the managing elite of the global economy and the latter created as a platform for the excluded and for victims of globalization. Davos now welcomes NGO and fair trade representatives. This is how Paola Ghiliani, director of the Max Havelaar foundation, was invited to the Davos forum in 2000, and chosen as one of the 100 "global leaders" of tomorrow. In 2005, Brazil's President Lula, founder of the country's Labor Party and one of alter-globalization's symbolic figures, traveled to Davos after having spoken at Porto Alegre. He said the following: "Included in this approach is the task of discussing possible common areas between the World Social Forum in Porto Alegre and the World Economic Forum in Davos, which is taking place at the same time. It is not a matter of asking people to stop being who they are but of establishing links between communities united by an indivisible human destiny" (Lula da Silva 2005).

In this context, it is interesting to compare Beck's ideas with the analyses of Michael Hardt and Antonio Negri (2001), since they are both symptomatic of an approach that radically challenges the nation-state concept. They observe that an all-inclusive entity is being put in place which the former identifies as a "cosmopolitical regime" and the latter define under the heading of "empire." To counterbalance the virtually totalitarian character of this new political form, Hardt and Negri, faithful to the Marxist tradition, base their hopes on deep movements that will allow the multitude to establish itself, while Beck, in the tradition of Habermas, banks on a project that will ensure the merging of democracy and human rights.

Curiously, both works conclude by referring to religion. Beck talks of cosmopolitanism as a "terrestrial religion" or a "secularized divine order," while the authors of *Empire* evoke the image of Saint Francis of Assisi. Similarly, they refer to the concept of love, peculiar to Christianity and Judaism, or "God's love of humanity and humanity's love of God" and decide on "the need to recover today this material and political sense of love, a love as strong as death" (Hardt and Negri 2004, 352). Such religious references, in theoretical constructions that are meant, above all, to be rational and analytical, seem to me symptomatic. Perhaps we should place them in a context marked by the difficulty of comprehending the power question. It is as though we were seeing a sort of evasion at the heart of critical thought, in the face of developments that seem constantly to propel it toward a future that its own categories can clarify only imperfectly.

Critical thought may, on the other hand, be literally blinded by the obvious omnipresence of that power (the "power without society") that reproduces itself without necessarily laying itself open, so that those who rally against it find themselves having to fall back on incantation. This situation is particularly noticeable among the alter-globalizationists—heirs to a rhetoric dominated by the concepts of society and state, who themselves admit the trouble they have redefining a strategy together. We will hardly be surprised, then, at the success of forums—spaces where the word reigns supreme, where endless discussions go on concerning changes in the world, where people come to recharge their batteries, express themselves, weigh the evils of the present and peer into a black future.

Are these true places of debate? Do people really gather here to produce decisions? I was going to say, "Certainly not!" given that it seems to me that forums—and even more so their online equivalents—are above all contexts for the trading of words. This great word market enters into a symmetrical relationship with the distant and mysterious powers of "the markets." These realms, which lie behind the decisions governing our daily lives, produce primarily figures—net results, the effects of which will be the creation, elimination, or relocation of jobs. But the great word market finds it harder to gear itself up for action: all that comes from it are stances and suggestions and a vague force which in contrast to the preceding period, is no longer oriented toward establishing a new world with a brighter future. In this context, it is not surprising that NGOs should want to get out—from a structurally double game—while the going is good. They are as much at ease in the domain of words as they are in the realism of action, where they have established a constructive partnership between the finance and the economy of survival.

We should not, however, seek to explain the rise in power of the NGO phenomenon as the end result of a successful combination of humanitarian ideology and a pragmatism that is always on alert to the sound and the fury of the world. Similarly, the place occupied today by transnational institutions such as the WTO, the UN, and the IMF is not merely the result of their functionality in the global system. In fact, we are witnessing a reconfiguration of the political domain which does not content itself with the development of governance exclusively centered on territoriality, any more than it implies the extinction of the nation-state—a world without sovereignty. This is why theories traditionally based on the dialectic between power and society focus on the change of scale (where is power situated and which is the relevant political space? etc.), in search of an impossible return to order and an unattainable harmony where the forces of society would recover control of this increasingly distant and mysterious power, making it possible to remedy imbalances and inequalities. These theoretical and political elaborations have in common that they all exist within a logic of harmonious living together (convivance), while the practices we are dealing with are unfolding in the context of survival. To use Michel Foucault's distinction, these practices fall within the "pastoral" dimension of pastoral power and apply less to "civil subjects" than to "living individuals."

If one can talk of global governmentality in reference to this constellation of transnational institutions and organizations, it is not in the sense of an inclusive reordering, like that of one power overlaying existing powers. This vision of things is part of the convivance perspective. Its final realization is "empire," a construction that falls within the same paradigm as the "state" of the philosophers—a form intended to organize the communal life of subject citizens. Yet, in societies where threat is an integral dimension of the present, questions of life and survival now appear much more fundamental—so ideas of balance and order, justice and law only make sense in the context of a precaution-oriented viewpoint.

It is no accident that the theme of sustainability is now so profoundly tied in with theories having to do with inequalities and the relationship between power and society. Thus, the Brazilian president, citing the frightening imbalance between the rich and poor countries, wrote, "Solidarity with life must always overcome the mechanisms of death. Debts must be honored, but payment must not mean the euthanasia of the debtor. The holders of the surplus of financial wealth must consider the social deficit afflicting three-quarters of humanity" (Lula da Silva 2005). Who is a debtor toward whom? Is it the poor person who has been given a loan by the rich person but is getting daily into deeper debt? Is it the rich person, laying down the law to the world and profiting from inequalities? In raising once more the issue of social deficit, Brazil's leader rubs salt into a wound. While advocating a vital rebalancing and a reorganization of society, he is referring explicitly to life ("solidarity with life") and death (the need to overcome the "mechanisms of death"). These terms, far from being innocuous, deserve our full attention. They refer back directly to the issue of harmonious living together (convivance), in the name of which he considers it impossible to stick to the traditional divides—by excluding himself from the Davos forum because he is one of the major figures of Porto Alegre. Symbolically, the terms of the theory and the stance that results from it thrust us into multidimensional issues—some will say into a problematic dualism—

since he explicitly admits that accepting the requirement of "solidarity with life" involves greater presence in the new centers of transnational politics.

The separation of living individuals and civil subjects highlighted by Foucault has, in our own historical context, led to the emergence of the issue of survival and its expression in a political space which, while it ties in with the traditional domain of "international relations," actually goes far beyond it. This space has become denser by internalizing anthropological anxiety in the face of an assortment of threats, ranging from terrorism to the planet's ecological vulnerability—while the nation-state form was unable to give a satisfactory answer to the question of human rights. Dialoguing with Habermas on the subject of terrorism and the events of September 11, Jacques Derrida (2004) compared the way death and destruction arise from within a society to an autoimmune process. Evil does not arise from the exterior, nor is it the fruit of contamination—life itself works to destroy its own defenses.

For this philosopher, what characterizes the retrospective perception of the events of September 11 is that they are experienced not just as an aggression (certainly violent, but in the past) but also as an opening onto an almost equally threatening future. "We are talking about a trauma, and thus an event, whose temporality proceeds neither from the now that is present nor from the present that is past but from an im-presentable to come" (Derrida 2004, 97). What is setting in is a fear of the worst—of bacteriological or even nuclear aggression. "Traumatism is produced by the future, by the to-come, by the threat of the worst to come, rather than by aggression that is 'over and done with'" (2004, 97). In this context, Derrida underlines the role that international institutions could have, "imperfect though they may be," and brings up the outlook of "a new figure, not necessarily in the form of the state, of universal sovereignty." Concerning what he himself describes as "utopian," the philosopher wonders if he should not describe this "ultimate form of sovereignty that would reconcile absolute justice with absolute law" as "god to come," and invoke, in connection, "messianicity without messianism" (2004, 156).

When Derrida links the idea of an international juridico-political space to a "to-come" (*a-venir*, a future) whose realization amounts to the "possibility of this impossible thing," this is not a matter of verbal caution. I tend to see in it rather the desire to bring to light the extraordinary difficulty of not flattening the new dimension of "global politics" by sticking to a purely institutionalist vision. Global politics casts us into a regime of anticipation and bears the hallmarks of the lack of fulfillment. It can neither be contained in terms of power balances nor thought of as a superstate form. It is developing alongside the world of territorial sharing, without imposing itself on states and on traditional regimes of sovereignty as an overarching power. *Between the nation-state and global politics we find the same polarity as that which exists between the regime of convivance and the regime of survival.* Today, global politics is, to a high degree, dependent on the strategies of nation-states. However, as the impact of initiatives dealing with the economy of survival show, it imposes its own system and puts under pressure those powers that control it only imperfectly.

One way of interpreting the way in which themes represented by the NGOs establish themselves is to conclude that global politics contaminates sovereignty. We can wonder about the anthropological implications of this bipolarity in our representation of power. At this point, it is useful to put this configuration in perspective, along with the observations of divine kingship. We saw to what extent the problematic of survival is central for these societies and the mechanism that they elaborated to protect themselves from the real and symbolic threats around them. It is the figure of the sovereign because he concentrates—in his excess, at the meeting point of nature and culture—the superpower that constitutes the guarantee of the universe's reproduction. At the same time, if we examine it from the perspective of convivance, the king occupies a precarious position—power is in fact under the control of the group.

Let us now turn to the way that the relationship to survival is managed in the global-political context. Here, we do not find an equivalent to divine kingship; there is no symbolic incarnation that concentrates power in order to resist the dangers menacing the planet. On the contrary, those who hold the most power in transnational organization are often anonymous to the public. With the exception of specialists, who knows the name of the head of the IMF, or the heads of organizations such as Amnesty International, the WWF, and Oxfam? In this sphere, we would not find one ounce of charisma. Moreover, transnational leaders are generally highly ranked technocrats instead of virtuosos of the political scene. It is the image of an undefined power, a nontransparent universe that prevails, a counterpoint of the "power without society" attributed to financial markets.

It is necessary to look elsewhere than in the representation of superpower to find the way that the relationship to survival is incarnated in the contemporary political sphere. In the great ritual of the reproduction of the world managed by the omnipresent figure of the divine king, we can oppose the recurrent spectacle of global anxiety in which the representatives of the people now participate. The Summit of the Earth in Rio (1992) inaugurated the kind of event where we display the goodwill acting to "assure a more secure and prosperous future." The application of Agenda 21, which aimed to promote sustainable development by reconciling development and ecosystem protection, gave rise to other conferences. The global summit of sustainable development in Johannesburg, ten years after Rio, was the occasion for considerable action. In addition to the representatives of the 173 countries present, NGOs and businesses participated at this ritual gathering, where the most powerful world leaders went to give speeches paved with good intentions. All of these people were concentrated in the biggest business center of South Africa, with a skyscraper's view of an enormous slum.

The media is a remarkable echo chamber for this kind of event. It is even more so when the great transnational conferences take place in hostile circumstances, as in the case of the WTO conference in Seattle (1999), when demonstrators blockaded the town. Tragedy can also be involved, as during the G8 meeting in Genoa (2001), when confrontations with the police led to the fatal shooting of a young man. In a completely different, but equally spectacular context, the huge concerts initiated by musician and producer Bob Geldof and others shine a harsh light on the ills that afflict the world and the dangers that threaten it. Here, all who wish to do so can take part in the group emotion in situ, unless they prefer sharing in it via television.

It is on quite varied levels, then, that we are seeing a group power take shape, made of tensions and even confrontations and rallying participants from widely diverse strata. These rallies have a highly variable content, since they can express the violence of dissent just as readily as they can give rise to the sort of humanitarian unanimity we saw in the days following the Asian Tsunami. In fact, we are dealing with performances, whose effect is to bring to the forefront of the political agenda issues which hitherto fell under the umbrella of ethics and religion. Natural disasters and humanitarian catastrophes give rise to what, once upon a time, was known as *l'horreur sacrée* (fear of divine retribution). Whether we claim modernity in this case changes nothing. The reflex that animates our fellow citizens is imprinted with a religious dimension that is quite real.

Rather than worldwide disillusionment, which some see as synonymous with modernity, perhaps the sacred is making a comeback and manifesting itself in charitable behavior and the predisposition to give. In this case, we should not see the magnitude of the charitable reaction as an epiphenomenon — a reaction entirely explicable by contextual factors — but take seriously the way in which the issue of survival is now establishing itself as a challenge of citizenship, globally as well as locally. That the anthropological anxiety focused on survival could lastingly reshape not only our perception of the world but also our modes of political action, by changing our priorities and generating new debates and totally new initiatives, provides food for thought to those currently wondering about the future of the relationship between the individual and the group and, beyond that, the political and the sacred.

This concrete expression of global politics on the emotional level sometimes seems like a kitsch stage performance, strangely hybrid thanks to the simultaneous presence of characters from different "scenes." The Davos forum brought together the President Lula, freshly arrived from Porto Alegre; Gordon Brown, the British chancellor of the exchequer; Benjamin Mkapa, the Tanzanian president; and Bill Gates, the richest man in the world. They were all together to lead one of the sessions dedicated to world poverty. Each in his respective role emphasized the lack of money to cure poverty in Africa, as well as sicknesses that, like malaria, kill thousands of children each day. They also complained of the inadequacy of developmental aid, in the absence of true political will.

The public, composed of economic summiteers, is listening politely when, all of a sudden, in the front rows, people start murmuring. Someone stands up. It is the actress Sharon Stone. "Mr. President," she says to Benjamin Mkapa, "I offer my help. I give $10,000 to buy mosquito nets." She proceeds to call on the speakers. Then, she turns toward the audience. "Stand up," she says, "Join me to help the Tanzanian president to save the children of his country." Very quickly, people begin to react. "I give $50,000," says one participant. Following him, others pledge to give as well. Numbers resonate in the air as during an auction. All the donors are now standing up and they are being applauded. Sharon Stone is beaming. An assistant passes through the audience to pick up business cards. In all, $1 million was gathered.[2]

Other celebrities were also present, including Peter Gabriel, Lionel Richie, and Richard Gere. Youssou N'Dour wrote a song on malaria. "We thought we'd been great at getting big names in business, politics and media, but not great at getting celebrities. It's a goldmine," said Claudia Gonzalez, one of the forum's organizers. They follow modestly in the wake of U2's Bono, the pioneer of global activism. What is certain is that we are communing in a ritual that trains the spotlight on the misery of the Third World and the ever-renewed struggle to ensure conditions favorable to sustainable development. What makes this kind of ritual so powerful is the plurality of the participants and the diversity of their sympathies, and the fact that the charisma lies not so much with political power as with artists. Global politics draws its efficacy from its capacity to evoke the outlook of survival in varied ways. Through performances ranging

2. And the actress commented: "I was there, and I heard that we were going to do this, that, taxes, initiatives, and I began to boil. I said to myself: this president needs money now, today. Mosquitoes are killing while we are talking. The people in this room have this money in their pockets. I want this money. It doesn't matter if people think I'm the volunteer service blond" (*Le Monde*, January 29, 2005).

from these charitable displays to great mass demonstrations, which also spark off the confrontation between the voices of the powerful and the poor, global politics highlights the world's precariousness and suggests possible initiatives and ways out by which we might remedy the catastrophic effects generated by the reproduction of our societies.

It is not by chance that the sacred dimension is present, to the degree that we can compare the rallies unleashed by the great catastrophes to veritable expiatory rituals. In encompassing uncertainty about the "to-come," global politics does not only call upon science and expertise—although these play an increasing role in organizations dealing with sustainable development and ways of defeating poverty. Hope and belief are also quite present in the emotions global politics give rise to. In associating the idea of a Coming God with a democratic future in which national state sovereignty is overtaken, Derrida, in his way, echoes the contradictions produced by globalized political space. In the perspective of convivance, however, the dissociation of the religious and the political finds its quintessence in the secular ideal of the separation between church and state (which claims to separate the world of belief and management of the polis); in the perspective of survival, this type of division becomes problematic. The crossover between sacred and profane can be seen in both great media ceremonies and in theories on globalization. As we have seen, adepts of the cosmopolitical or alter idea are quick to evoke paradise on earth or the figure of Saint Francis of Assisi.

The complexity of global politics means we cannot just see it as a substitute for existing politics. Those who have tried to think through and promote the overtaking of the nation-state, using concepts or constitutional formulas, so far have gotten nowhere. Today, alongside the political places of sovereignty organized around the institutional division of executive and legislative, another space is emerging where the legitimacy of a decision-making monopoly becomes increasingly blurred.

For anthropologists, this type of political place is generally distinguished by the lack of separation between "within" and "without." The technical nature of the material dealt with, however, tends to give rise precisely to such a separation. Similarly, during global conferences, enclosing the negotiators on a stage of grand palaces and subjecting them to continual surveillance reinforces the feeling of a divide between the elite and the outside world. In Cancun, as in Seattle, however, it is no accident that we see pressure groups from the four corners of the earth converging on the negotiating site. This massive presence is a major factor in modifying our spontaneous perception of a world where political and diplomatic initiative is the exclusive right of a minority that holds all power and knowledge. This aspect attracts insufficient attention from specialist observers, who focus more on the spectacle of the dispute and on its media figureheads.

It is time to modify our vision of politics, obscured as it is by the search for a predominant and omnipotent political "place." On the contrary, what is actually evolving is a set of systems that undermine the perception of sovereignty that has long been the foundation of Western governmental practices.

Conclusion

I am aware, at the end of this book, of having devoted myself to an unusual exploration for an anthropologist. This exploration combines the present and the future in a domain where one generally measures only the present in light of the past, of the long and even very long duration. In my defense, I must note that it is difficult to analyze the political in our societies without being seized by notions and debates often preconstructed by political actors and their accredited witnesses. That explains my propensity for putting several prospects into play, and for sometimes giving the good role to philosophers and ethnographers. But, above all, this has led me to construct an approach that takes into account — in all their plasticity — original structures such as the European Union or nongovernmental organizations, and the real effects that they produce as part of a dynamic process where the virtual seems encrusted in the present. I call this approach *cultural anticipation*, which imposes itself on the anthropologist when he is interested in a field both contemporary in time and close in space. Cultural anticipation makes it possible to seize the work of the real by emancipating oneself, at least partially, from certain optical illusions related to the observer's familiarity with the object of his object.

Under these conditions it should not be surprising that I updated the problematic of survival, a little like the visible part of an iceberg whose extension and depth is still difficult to comprehend. At the beginning, it seemed reductive to treat the displacement of the political as a simple consequence of globalization. My own observations on the European Union and transnational organisms and organizations led me to reflect on what distinguishes survival as a mode of action and to highlight the specificity of global-politics. In regard to conceptions anchored in an episteme of harmoniously living together (convivance), global-politics can seem like a somewhat monstrous hybrid, incorporating heterogeneous experiences, without reestablishing an encompassing and coherent order. Must one, however, seek at all costs to reproduce on a vaster scale the type of mechanism that was essential during an altogether relatively limited period of the history of humanity? Admittedly, the question of a new world order often arises in the discourse of political leaders. But this obsession with a global rearrangement in the name of a community of values seems more and more askew in relation to the major concerns of our fellow citizens. And if they have definitively finished their mourning of a demiurgic vision of politics, they are not thus satisfied to be left to the whims of a dubious economic situation. It is undoubtedly the reason for which pragmatic discourses are hardly more successful than the invocation of great principles.

With global politics, the issue now on the agenda is a politics of survival—and this is being expressed in varied ways in public space. The fact that the problem of survival is now at the center of our ways of practicing and thinking about today's politics is a new factor in this young century, whose full implications have not yet become apparent. The fact that fear of the unknown can transform politics at the deepest level, that the sense of threat people feel should become a major torment in our societies, that the political ideal should shape parliamentary business (and not vice versa) by causing a rise in the power of transnational operations, that collective aspirations and even individual electoral behavior should be determined by the precautionary principle—these are all factors that should impel us to update our analytical grids and ways of acting. Odds are that the period now beginning will expand this approach to politics. Will the undercurrent end up changing the rules of the game and changing the hierarchies currently found in the corridors of power? Or, conversely, might the governing powers adapt gently, making ample space for requirements they once considered marginal? It is too soon to claim that we can answer these questions. What is certain, though, is that it will not be long before we see the full impact of the virtualities contained within the politics of survival.

Bibliography

Abélès, Marc. 1992. *La Vie quotidienne au Parlement européen*. Paris: Hachette.

———. 2002. *Les Nouveaux riches: Un Éthnologue dans la Silicon Valley*. Paris: Odile Jacob.

Abensour, Miguel. 1997. *La Démocratie contre l'Etat*. Paris: PUF.

Adler, Alfred. 1982. *La Mort est le masque du roi: La royauté sacrée chez les Moundang du Tchad*. Paris: Payot.

Agamben, Giorgio. 1998. *Homo Sacer: Sovereign Power and Bare Life*. Translated by Daniel Heller-Roazen. Stanford, Calif.: Stanford University Press.

———. 2000. *Means without Ends: Notes on Politics*. Translated by Vincenzo Binetti and Cesare Casarino. Minneapolis: University of Minnesota Press.

Agulhon, Maurice. 1989. *Marianne au pouvoir*. Paris: Flammarion.

Anheier, Helmut K., and Lester M. Salamon. 1996. *The Emerging Nonprofit Sector: A Comparative Analysis*. Manchester: Manchester University Press.

Antelme, Robert. 1998 [1957]. *The Human Race*. Translated by Jeffrey Haight and Annie Mahler. Evanston, Ill.: Marlboro Press/Northwestern.

Appadurai, Arjun. 1996. *Modernity at Large: Cultural Dimensions of Globalization*. Minneapolis: University of Minnesota Press.

Arendt, Hannah. 1968. *Totalitarianism: Part Three of "The Origins of Totalitarianism."* New York: Harvest Books.

———. 1973. *The Origins of Totalitarianism.* New York: Harcourt Brace Jovanovich.

———. 1992 [1963]. *Eichmann in Jerusalem: A Report on the Banality of Evil.* New York: Penguin Classics.

Arts, Bas. 2003/4. *Non-State Actors in Global Governance: Three Faces of Power.* Preprints aus der Max-Planck-Projektgruppe Recht der Gemeinschaftsgüter, Bonn.

Badie, Bertrand. 1995. *La Fin des territoires.* Paris: Fayard.

———. 1999. *Un Monde sans souveraineté.* Paris: Fayard.

———. 2004. *L'impuissance de la puissance.* Paris: Fayard.

Balandier, Georges. 1985. *Le Détour.* Paris: Fayard.

———. 1988. *Le Désordre: Éloge du mouvement.* Paris: Fayard.

Bauman, Zygmunt. 2004. *Wasted Lives: Modernity and its Outcasts.* Oxford: Polity Press.

Bayart, Jean-François. 2004. *Le Gouvernement du monde.* Paris: Fayard.

Beattie, J. 1959. "Rituals of Nyoro Kingship." *Africa* 29:134–45.

Beck, Ulrich. 1992. *Risk Society: Towards a New Modernity.* London: Sage.

———. 2003. *Pouvoir et contre-pouvoir à l'ère de la mondialisation.* Paris: Aubier.

Bellier, Irène. 1995. "Morality, Language, and Power in European Institutions." *Social Anthropology* 3 (3): 235–50.

Benjamin, Walter. 2002 [1940]. "Paralipomena to 'On the Concept of History.'" In *Selected Writings*, vol. 4, *1938–1940*, edited by Howard Eiland and Michael W. Jennings; translated by Edmund Jephcott et al., 401–11. Cambridge, Mass.: Belknap/Harvard University Press.

Bettati, Mario, and Bernard Kouchner. 1987. *Le Devoir d'ingérence: Peut-on les laisser mourir?* Paris: Denoël.

Biersteker, Thomas, and Rodney Hall. 2001. "L'Émergence des autorités privées." *Alternatives économiques* 47:17–19.

Bloch, Ernst. 1986 [1967]. *The Principle of Hope.* Cambridge, Mass.: MIT Press.

Bradbury, R. E. 1967. "The Kingdom of Benin." In *West African Kingdoms in the Nineteenth Century*, edited by D. Ford and P. M. Kaberry. London: Oxford University Press.

Brauman, Rony. 2002 [1996]. *Humanitaire: Le dilemme*. Paris: Textuel.

Cahiers Français. 2001. "ONG et Mondialisation." Paris: La Documentation Française, 305.

Callon, Michel, Pierre Lascoumes, and Yannick Barthe. 2001. *Agir dans un monde incertain: Essai sur la démocratie technique*. Paris: Seuil.

Canetti, Elias. 1984 [1947]. *Auto-da-Fé*. Translated by D. V. Wedgewood. New York: Farrar, Straus and Giroux.

———. 1984 [1962]. *Crowds and Power*. Translated by Carol Stuart. New York: Farrar, Straus and Giroux.

Castel, Robert. 2003. *L'Insécurité sociale*. Paris: Seuil.

Castells, Manuel. 2001 [1996]. *The Rise of the Network Society*. Malden, Mass.: Blackwell.

Cohen, Daniel. 2004. *La Mondialisation et ses ennemis*. Paris: Grasset.

Cohen, Samy. 2003. *La Résistance des États: Les Démocraties face aux défis de la mondialisation*. Paris: Seuil.

Constant, Benjamin. 1980. *De la liberté des anciens chez les modernes*. Paris: Hachette-Pluriel.

Croisat, Maurice, and Jean-Louis Quermonne. 1996. *L'Europe et le fédéralisme*. Paris: Montchrestien.

Cuillerai, Marie. 2002. *Le Capitalisme vertueux*. Paris: Payot.

———. 2003. "Le Réel par effraction: Qu'est-ce qu'une intervention économique?" Conference, Autour de "l'intervention": Protagonistes, logiques, effets. University of Montreal, October 23–25.

Das, Veena, and Deborah Poole, eds. 2004. *Anthropology in the Margins of the State*. Santa Fe, N.M.: School of American Research.

de Heusch, Luc. 1958. *Essais sur le symbolisme de l'inceste royal en Afrique*. Brussels: Institut d'ethnologie de Solvay.

Deleuze, Gilles, and Félix Guattari. 1972. *Anti-Œdipus*. Translated by Robert Hurley, Mark Seem, and Helen R. Lane. London: Continuum.

Derrida, Jacques. 2004. "Autoimmunity: Real and Symbolic Suicides."

In *Philosophy in a Time of Terror: Dialogues with Jürgen Habermas and Jacques Derrida*, with Giovanna Borradori, 85–136. Chicago: University of Chicago Press.

Dezalay, Yves, and Bryant G. Garth. 1996. *Dealing in Virtue: International Commercial Arbitration and the Construction of a Transnational Legal Order*. Chicago: University of Chicago Press.

Douglas, Mary. 1963. *The Lele of the Kasai*. London: Oxford University Press.

Dupin, Eric. 2005. "Deux France caricaturales." *Les Echos*, May 27.

Dupuy, Jean-Pierre. 2002. *Avions-nous oublié le mal? Penser la politique après le 11 septembre*. Paris: Bayard.

Engels, Frederick. 1990 [1884]. "The Origin of Family, Private Property, and the State." In *Collected Works*, vol. 26, *Frederick Engels, 1882–89*, by Karl Marx and Frederick Engels, 129–276. London: Lawrence and Wishart.

Evans-Pritchard, E. E. 1966 [1940]. "The Nuer of Southern Sudan." In *African Political Systems*, edited by E. E. Evans-Pritchard and M. Fortes, 272–96. Oxford: Oxford University Press.

Foucault, Michel. 1976. *La Volonté de savoir*. Paris: Gallimard.

———. 1984. "Polemics, Politics, and Problematizations." In *The Foucault Reader*, edited by Paul Rabinow, 381–90. New York: Pantheon.

———. 1997. *Il faut défendre la société: Cours au Collège de France, 1975–1976*. Paris: Gallimard, Seuil.

———. 2000a. "Omnes et Singulatim." In *Essential Works of Foucault, 1954–1984*, vol. 3, *Power*, edited by James Faubion, 298–325. New York: New Press.

———. 2000b. "The Subject and Power." In *Essential Works of Foucault, 1954–1984*, vol. 3, *Power*, edited by James Faubion, 326–48. New York: New Press.

———. 2001. "Cours du 14 janvier 1976." In *Dits et écrits*, vol. 2, *1976–1988*, 175–89. Paris: Gallimard.

Frazer, James. 1925. *The Golden Bough*. Abridged ed. London: Macmillan.

Gauchet, Marcel. 1997. *The Disenchantment of the World*. Translated by Oscar Burge. Princeton: Princeton University Press.

————. 2002. *La Démocratie contre elle-même*. Paris: Gallimard.

Giddens, Anthony. 2002. "The Globalizing Modernity." In *The Global Transformation Reader: An Introduction to the Globalization Debate*, edited by David Held and Anthony G. McGrew, 60–66. Cambridge: Polity Press.

Gilroy, Paul. 2004. *After Empire: Multiculture or Postcolonial Melancholia*. London: Routledge.

Godelier, Maurice. 1984. *L'idéel et le matériel*. Paris: Fayard.

Guilhot, Nicolas. 2004. *Wall Street ou les fortunes de la vertu*. Paris: Raisons d'agir.

Gupta, Akhil, and Aradhana Sharma. 2006. "Globalization and Postcolonial States." *Current Anthropology* 47 (2): 277–307.

Haas, Ernest. 1958. *The Uniting of Europe: Political, Economic and Social Forces, 1950–1957*. Stanford, Calif.: Stanford University Press.

Habermas, Jürgen. 2000. *The Postnational Constellation*. Translated by Max Pensky. Cambridge: Polity Press.

Hardt, Michael, and Antonio Negri. 2001. *Empire*. Cambridge, Mass: Harvard University Press.

————. 2004. *Multitude: War and Democracy in the Age of Empire*. New York: Penguin Press.

Hartog, François. 2003. *Régimes d'historicité: Présentisme et expérience du temps*. Paris: Seuil.

Harvey, David. 1990. *The Condition of Postmodernity: An Enquiry into the Origin of Cultural Change*. Cambridge, Mass.: Blackwell.

Hermitte, Marie-Angèle. 2001. "Pouvoirs sur la vie, pouvoirs sur la mort, les rôles du droit." In *Qu'est-ce que l'humain?* edited by Yves Michaud, 539–48. Paris: Odile Jacob.

Hocart, A. M. 1970 [1936]. *Kings and Councillors*. Chicago: University of Chicago Press.

Hume, David. 1992. *Treatise of Human Nature*. New York: Prometheus Books.

Jameson, Fredric. 1984. "Postmodernism or the Cultural Logic of Late Capitalism." *New Left Review* 146:53–92.

Jaouani, Salim. 2002. "Le Partenariat ONG-multinationales." *Les Echos*, February 12.

Jennar, Raoul M. 2004. *Europe, la trahison des élites*. Paris: Fayard.

Jonas, Hans. 1990 [1979]. *Le Principe responsabilité*. Paris: Éditions du Cerf.

Kantorowicz, Ernst. 1957. *The King's Two Bodies*. Princeton: Princeton University Press.

Keohane, Robert O., and Stanley Hoffmann. 1991. *The New European Community*. Boulder, Colo.: Westview Press.

Koselleck, Reinhart. 2004 [1979]. *Futures Past: On the Semantics of Historical Time*. Translated by Keith Tribe. New York: Columbia University Press.

Kuper, Hilda. 1947. *An African Aristocracy: Rank among the Swazi*. London: Oxford University Press.

Lamy, Pascal. 2004. *La Démocratie-monde: Pour une autre gouvernance globale*. Paris: Seuil.

Lefort, Claude. 1986. *Essais sur le politique: XIXe–XXe siècles*. Paris: Seuil.

Lévi-Strauss, Claude. 1950. Preface to *Sociologie et anthropologie*, by Marcel Mauss. Paris: PUF.

———. 1983. "Histoire et ethnologie." *Annales* 6:1217–31.

———. 1998. "Retours en arrière." *Les Temps modernes* 598:66–69.

Lula da Silva, Luiz Inácio. 2005. "Entre Davos et Porto Alegre, des champs communs possibles." *Le Monde*, January 27.

Manent, Pierre. 1995 [1987]. *An Intellectual History of Liberalism*. Translated by Rebecca Balinski. Princeton: Princeton University Press.

Manin, Bernard. 1997. *Principles of Representative Government*. Cambridge: Cambridge University Press.

Massiah, Gustave. 2000. "ONG et mondialisation, quelles perspectives après Seattle?" AITEC website. http://www.globenet.org/aitec/contributions/ongmond.htm.

Mauss, Marcel. 1990 [1950]. *The Gift: The Form and Reason for Exchange in Archaic Societies*. Translated by W. D. Halls. London: Routledge.

Meek, Charles. 1931. *A Sudanese Kingdom*. London: Kegan and Paul.

Mény, Yves, et al. 1995. *Politiques publiques en Europe*. Paris: L'Harmattan.

Monnet, Jean. 1976. *Mémoires*. Paris: Fayard.

Muller, Jean-Claude. 1980. *Le Roi bouc émissaire: Pouvoir et rituel chez les Rukuba du Nigéria central*. Quebec: S. Fleury.

Ong, Aiwha. 1999. *Flexible Citizenship: The Cultural Logics of Transnationality*. Durham, N.C.: Duke University Press.

Pandolfi, Mariella. 2002. "'Moral entrepreneurs,' souverainetés mouvantes et barbelés." *Anthropologie et Sociétés* 26 (1): 29–51.

Perrot, Cl.-H. 1982. *Les Anyi-Ndénié et le pouvoir aux XVIIIe et XIXe siècles*. Paris: Éditions de la Sorbonne.

Pomyan, Krysztof. 1980. "La Crise de l'avenir." *Le Débat* 7:5–17.

Rancière, Jacques. 2000. "Biopolitique ou politique? Entretien recueilli par Eric Alliez." *Multitudes* website. Posted March 2000.

———. 2002. *La Mésentente*. Paris: Galilée.

Richards, Audrey I. 1968. "Keeping the King Divine." *Proceedings of the Royal Anthropological Institute*: 22–35.

Robertson, Roland. 1992. *Globalization: Social Theory and Global Culture*. London: Sage.

Rosanvallon, Pierre. 1998. *Le Peuple introuvable: Histoire de la représentation démocratique en France*. Paris: Gallimard.

———. 2000. *The New Social Question*. Translated by Barbara Harshav. Princeton: Princeton University Press.

Roscoe, John. 1968. *The Bakitara of the Banyoro*. Cambridge: Cambridge University Press.

Rosenau, James. 1990. *Turbulence in World Politics*. New York: Harvester.

Rosenau, James, and E. O. Czempiel. 1992. *Governance without Government: Order and Change in World Politics*. Cambridge: Cambridge University Press.

Sassen, Saskia. 1998. *Globalization and Its Discontents*. New York: New Press.

Schuman, Robert. 1950. *Declaration*. French Minister of Foreign Affaires, Quai d'Orsay, Salon de l'Horloge, Paris. May 9. Available at the Robert Schuman Foundation website, http://www.robert-schuman.eu/declaration_9mai.php.

Seligman, C. G. 1934. *Egypt and Negro Africa: A Study of Divine Kingship*. London: Routledge.

Shiva, Vandana. 1991. *Ecology and the Politics of Survival: Conflicts over Natural Resources in India*. New Delhi: Sage.

Shore, Cris, and Annabel Black. 1994. "Citizen's Europe and the Construction of European Identity." In *The Anthropology of Europe: Identities and Boundaries in Conflict*, edited by V. A. Goddard, J. R. Llobera, and C. Shore, 275–98. London: Berg Press.

Strange, Susan. 1996. *The Retreat of the State: The Diffusion of Power in World Economy*. Cambridge: Cambridge University Press,

Sur, Serge. 1999. "La Convention de Rome entre ONG et Conseil de sécurité." *Revue générale de droit international public*, January–March.

Taguieff, P. A. 2000. *L'Ère des traces*. Paris: Galilée.

Thiry, Bernard. 1994. "Rapport introductif." In *Actes du Forum européen des acteurs sociaux sur les Services d'intérêt général*. Brussels, November 25–26.

Trouillot, Michel-Rolph. 2003. *Global Transformations: Anthropology and the Modern World*. New York: Palgrave-Macmillan.

Vansina, Jan. 1954. "Les Valeurs culturelles des Bushong." *Zaïre* 8 (9): 899–910.

———. 1955. "Initiation Rituals of the Bushong." *Africa* 25:138–53.

Willetts, Peter. 2000. "From 'Consultative Arrangements' to 'Partnership': The Changing Status of NGOs in Diplomacy at the UN." *Global Governance* 6:191–212.

Young, Michael W. 1966. "The Divine Kingship of the Jukun: A Reevaluation of Some Theories." *Africa* 36:135–52.

Zabusky, Stacia. 2000. "Boundaries at Work: Discourses and Practices of Belonging in the European Space Agency." In *An Anthropology of the European Union*, edited by Irène Bellier and Thomas M. Wilson, 179–200. Oxford: Berg Press.

Zonabend, Françoise. 1985. *The Enduring Memory: Time and History in a French Village*. Translated by Anthony Forster. Manchester: Manchester University Press.

Index

Marc Abélès is the director of research at the Centre National
de la Recherche Scientifique (CNRS) and the director of studies
at L'École des Hautes Études en Sciences Sociales (L'EHESS) in Paris.
He is the author of numerous books, including *Anthropologie de la
globalisation*, *Le Spectacle du pouvoir*, and *Quiet Days in Burgundy:
A Study of Local Politics*.

Julie Kleinman is a Ph.D. candidate in anthropology at
Harvard University.